NEW DIRECTIONS FOR CHILD DEVELOPMENT

William Damon, *Brown University*
EDITOR-IN-CHIEF

The Legacy of Lawrence Kohlberg

Dawn Schrader
Cornell University

EDITOR

Number 47, Spring 1990

JOSSEY-BASS INC., PUBLISHERS
San Francisco • Oxford

The Legacy of Lawrence Kohlberg.
Dawn Schrader (ed.).
New Directions for Child Development, no. 47.

NEW DIRECTIONS FOR CHILD DEVELOPMENT
William Damon, Editor-in-Chief

Copyright © 1990 by Jossey-Bass Inc., Publishers
and
Jossey-Bass Limited

Copyright under International, Pan American, and Universal Copyright Conventions. All rights reserved. No part of this issue may be reproduced in any form—except for a brief quotation (not to exceed 500 words) in a review or professional work—without permission in writing from the publishers.

NEW DIRECTIONS FOR CHILD DEVELOPMENT is part of The Jossey-Bass Social and Behavioral Science Series and is published quarterly by Jossey-Bass Inc., Publishers (publication number USPS 494-090). Second-class postage paid at San Francisco, California, and at additional mailing offices. Postmaster: Send address changes to Jossey-Bass Inc., Publishers, 350 Sansome Street, San Francisco, California 94104.

EDITORIAL CORRESPONDENCE should be sent to the Editor-in-Chief, William Damon, Department of Education, Box 1938, Brown University, Providence, Rhode Island 02912.

Library of Congress Catalog Card Number LC 85-644581

International Standard Serial Number ISSN 0195-2269

International Standard Book Number ISBN 1-55542-824-X

Cover photograph by Wernher Krutein. Copyright © 1990 PHOTOVAULT.
Manufactured in the United States of America. Printed on acid-free paper.

Contents

Editor's Notes 1
Dawn Schrader

1. The Role of Gender Identity and Gender Constancy in Sex-Differentiated Development 5
Eleanor E. Maccoby
Kohlberg's early writings provided the grounding for current conceptions of gender identity and gender constancy.

2. The Gender Concept Development Legacy 21
Ronald G. Slaby
The gender category system is presented as a prototype of all social-cognitive category systems.

3. Moral Judgment, Action, and Development 31
Elliot Turiel
The relationship between moral judgment and moral action as Kohlberg defined it is extended to include more comprehensive social psychological factors.

4. Kohlberg's Theory and Moral Motivation 51
Augusto Blasi
Kohlberg's position that moral understanding and moral reasoning provide motivation for moral action is contrasted with traditional conceptions of motivation.

5. Universality and Particularity 59
Lawrence Blum
Kohlberg's multiple views on the universality of moral reasoning are highlighted. Attention to particular situations and individuals is presented as an important aspect of morality.

6. A Story for Larry 71
Eleanor Duckworth, Joanne Cleary
A third-grade classroom illustrates the utilization of children's real-life moral dilemmas as an opportunity for moral education.

7. The Prison as a Just Community 77
Kelsey Kauffman
A prison provides the setting for examining underlying principles of the just community approach to moral education.

8. Kohlberg's Educational Legacy　　　　　　　　　　　　　　　　81
Fritz K. Oser
Principles of discourse underlying the just community approach to moral education are outlined in the context of a German school.

9. Some Personal Reflections on Larry Kohlberg as a Teacher of Teachers　　　　　　　　　　　　　　　　89
Edwin Fenton
A former colleague recounts his conversations and interactions with Kohlberg.

10. Lawrence Kohlberg's Socratic Paradox　　　　　　　　　　　　93
Wolfgang Edelstein
An analogy is drawn between Kohlberg and Socrates in the substance and procedure of moral education in the public sphere.

11. Moral Education Beyond Moral Reasoning　　　　　　　　　　99
Israel Scheffler
Three elements of Kohlberg's work contribute to the opening of a new level of dialogue between philosophers and psychologists.

INDEX　　　　　　　　　　　　　　　　　　　　　　　　　　103

Editor's Notes

> Will the future ever arrive? Should we continue to look upward? Will the light that we see in the sky soon be extinguished? The ideal is terrifying to behold, lost as it is in the depths; small, isolated, a pinpoint, brilliant but threatened on all sides by the dark forces that surround it. Nevertheless, in the end it is no more endangered than a star in the jaws of the clouds.
>
> —Victor Hugo

This volume commemorates Lawrence Kohlberg (1927-1987), educator, psychologist, and philosopher. His developmental theory, research program, and educational practices began a dialogue that expanded and strengthened our conceptions of morality. Yet Kohlberg's legacy reaches beyond traditional areas of inquiry in moral psychology. Grounding his theory in the writings of Piaget, Kohlberg addressed conceptions of justice, cross-cultural universality of moral judgments, gender identity and sex-typed behavior, motivation, moral education, and the relationship between moral judgment and moral action. The contributions in this volume of New Directions for Child Development exemplify the influence of Kohlberg's revolutionary ideas on eleven scholars in four areas of Kohlberg's research: gender identification, universality of moral judgment, moral reasoning and conduct, and moral education.

The present volume departs from the usual style of the New Directions series. Each chapter originally was presented at a symposium at the Harvard Graduate School of Education on April 15, 1988—one year after Kohlberg's death. The speakers invited to this symposium were all intellectually influenced by Kohlberg, although their individual scholarly pursuits are not always directly associated with Kohlberg's moral development theory. Some of the chapters are personal, anecdotal, and narrative in tone, providing a rare glimpse of Lawrence Kohlberg as a person as well as a scholar; others are critical or analytical; still others represent extensions or modifications of or reactions to Kohlberg's work. The unique style of each author has been preserved in this volume in order to provide texture and dimension to the breadth of Kohlberg's influence. The chapters also reveal Kohlberg's unique effect on his family of colleagues—both close and extended—in terms of their scholarship, their careers, and their lives. Herein lies Kohlberg's greatest legacy: the study of morality is a collaborative venture in which a community, in the truest sense of the word, joins in mind and spirit to create something larger than itself.

Certainly Kohlberg had his critics, some of whose views are contained in this volume. But even for his critics, Kohlberg's ideas warrant consideration and provide a starting point for development of new ideas. Kohlberg welcomed dialogue and controversy. He believed that without cognitive conflict and dialogue, we cease to develop.

This volume represents such dialogue. Each contributor addresses Kohlberg's influence on his or her own work. First, Eleanor Maccoby reviews her and her colleagues' research on the psychological implications of gender identification and the ways in which Kohlberg's 1966 paper foreshadowed new developments and insights in this area of study. Ronald G. Slaby comments on the influences of Maccoby and Kohlberg on the development of the social-cognitive development paradigm and on gender concept category systems.

Next, Elliot Turiel addresses the oft-made criticism that Kohlberg did not study moral action and outlines Kohlberg's myriad contributions to the understanding of judgment-action relationships—critical areas of inquiry even among those who do not hold a cognitive developmental perspective. Turiel points out that Kohlberg's "almost exclusive emphasis on the moral aspects of social interactions" obscured his vision of other significant social factors influencing action. Augusto Blasi adds to Turiel's discussion by responding to criticism that Kohlberg did not address moral motivation. Blasi articulates Kohlberg's conception that moral reasoning itself is motivating, and that by holding true to this conception, Kohlberg revolutionized the ways in which these problems are examined.

Lawrence Blum addresses Kohlberg's view of universality in moral reasoning and discusses how the conception of particularity, that is, attention to particular aspects of persons, contexts, and emotions, is an essential component of moral reasoning.

The volume concludes with six short chapters presenting different facets of Kohlberg's moral education programs. The first three examine Kohlberg's influence on individuals in various settings. Eleanor Duckworth and Joanne Cleary tell a story of how real-life moral problems promote moral development in elementary school children; Kelsey Kauffman relates her experiences with Kohlberg's just community approach with a prison population; and Fritz K. Oser relates his experiences instituting the just community approach to moral education in a German secondary school. The next two chapters give us a glimpse of Kohlberg as a moral educator. Edwin Fenton paints a portrait of Kohlberg as a teacher, colleague, and friend who was successful in conveying, in word and in deed, that the real purpose of working with students is respect for the students themselves, not research agendas. Wolfgang Edelstein likens Kohlberg to Socrates in both substance and procedure, pointing out paradoxes faced in implementing moral education curricula in current society.

Finally, Israel Scheffler discusses Kohlberg's influences in moral philosophy, moral development, and moral education and points to the future of moral education as extending beyond moral content to moral action.

The hope is that this volume stimulates continued thinking about moral issues, not only maintaining the dialogue between philosophers, psychologists, and educators but also developing new ideas and controversy and, most especially, moving toward the goal of a just, peaceful, and benevolent society and world. This is the legacy of Lawrence Kohlberg.

The symposium on which this volume is based was sponsored by Dean Patricia Albjerg Graham, Harvard University Graduate School of Education, and by the Harvard Center for Moral Education, which Kohlberg directed. I thank them for their sponsorship. I also thank Cliff Baden and the Programs in Professional Education staff for organizing the symposium, William Damon for chairing the symposium committee, and the symposium committee for designing the program. The committee members were William Damon, Mary Louise Arnold, Cliff Baden, Roger Brown, Ann Higgins, Gil Noam, Dawn Schrader, and Robert Selman. I am grateful as well to the hundreds of people who came from throughout the country and the world to share in the dialogue of that day. The comments made by the audience members were addressed in a number of the papers included in this volume.

I thank William Damon for the invitation to edit this volume and for his expertise and support. I especially thank Lawrence Kohlberg, in memoriam, for his friendship, his vision, and ultimately, his legacy.

Dawn Schrader
Editor

Dawn Schrader is assistant professor of educational psychology at Cornell University. Her chief research interests involve the understanding of the role of metacognition in the moral reasoning development and actions of adolescents and adults.

Kohlberg's 1966 challenge to the dominant theories concerning gender development influences current research in the field.

The Role of Gender Identity and Gender Constancy in Sex-Differentiated Development

Eleanor E. Maccoby

Upon rereading Kohlberg's 1966 paper on children's sex-role concepts and attitudes, I am struck by how well it stands the test of time. From today's perspective, it is difficult to realize how revolutionary the paper was for its time. In the early sixties, when it was written, there were two dominant theories about the gender aspects of development. Versions of learning theory stemming from Hull or Skinner probably had the strongest following. Learning theory was just beginning to be transformed into *social* learning theory through the added emphasis on observational learning or imitation, but the framework lacked the cognitive emphasis it has since acquired. Psychoanalytic theory was learning theory's main competitor. Kohlberg presented a theory that explicitly departed from both of the dominant views at that time.

Kohlberg in 1966: Departure From Then-Current Themes

Let us recall some of Kohlberg's statements in that remarkable 1966 paper. He argued that children's gender concepts are constructed, not directly taught. He claimed that fairly universal body imagery contributed to core gender schemas, but he parted company with the Freudians in his belief that the relevant images were not genital in nature but rather derived from adult gender differences in size and strength. He believed that gender concepts change in orderly ways over a considerable developmental time span, and that these changes are linked to general cognitive growth. While he noted that individual children differ in their rate of progress through the series of developmental steps, he did not think that different children took essentially different paths. Thus, he did not believe that variations among families in the degree and kind of sex-role socialization pressures they imposed had much power to shape children's sex role acquisitions differentially, at least not in comparison to the power of developmental forces impinging on all children. He distinguished gender identity from other aspects of children's understandings about the sex-linked characteristics of self and others. He viewed the formation of gender schemas, particularly identity schemas, as prior processes that motivate children to imitate same-sex others and to value and adopt whatever activities are deemed sex-appropriate in their respective cultures.

One of the most controversial points of this work dealt with the role of reinforcement. Social learning theorists argued that reinforcement and punishment were basic processes whereby children acquired sex-typed behavior, and that differential development of boys and girls could be traced to their having been reinforced or punished for different things. Kohlberg turned this process around, claiming that gender identity was a cognitive categorizing of the self and that this self-concept, once formed, then determined what would be rewarding to a child. Thus, for Kohlberg even reinforcement became to some degree a consequence rather than a cause of sex typing. Specifically, he claimed that the establishment of a firm gender identity would make children more susceptible to reinforcement by same-sex others. Thus, he anticipated by more than twenty years a paper by Fagot (1985) in which boys' behavior was shown to be influenced by the "reinforcements" provided by other boys, not by those provided by girls or by teachers, whereas girls' behavior was influenced by the reactions of teachers and of other girls, not by those of boys.

While nowadays there is by no means general agreement with all of these ideas that Kohlberg enunciated nearly twenty-five years ago, it is safe to say that some of them are now widely taken for granted. Gender schema theories now have a wide currency (for example, Bem, 1981), and as the cognitive revolution has spread through all walks of academic psychology, Kohlberg's writings seem central to the discipline, not peripheral as they once did. It is true that support for the hard version of stage theory has waned, and most current scholars no doubt believe in a greater degree of domain specificity in cognitive development than Kohlberg espoused. But a good deal of evidence has accumulated to support several aspects of Kohlberg's account.

Gender Constancy

Kohlberg's work on gender constancy has probably excited more attention and controversy than any other aspect of his theory. He said, "The child's gender identity can provide a stable organizer of the child's psychosexual attitudes only when he is categorically certain of its unchangeability" (1966, p. 95). He also said that children acquire gender constancy at about the same age as that identified by Piaget as typical for acquiring constancy (conservation) of such properties of physical objects as their mass, weight, and number. With DeVries (1969), Kohlberg conducted a study of "species constancy" and found that four-year-olds believed that a cat could change into a dog if its whiskers were cut off or if it wore a dog mask, whereas by age six or seven, they did not believe the cat's species identity could be changed in this way. Kohlberg saw the achievement of species constancy and gender constancy as closely linked: "The process of forming a constant gender identity is not a unique process determined by instinctual wishes and identifications, but a part of the general process of conceptual growth" (p. 98).

Kohlberg was not very clear about the age at which gender identity is sufficiently established to become the basis for sex typing. He cited DeLucia's (1963) work on toy preference with children of kindergarten age—who were thus at the lower bound for establishment of gender constancy—and noted that toy preferences were firmly established by this age. He referred to the work of Money, Hampson, and Hampson (1957) and agreed with them that gender identity becomes firmly established relatively early in life, and thereafter becomes very difficult to change. He did not agree, however, with their view that this process reflects a critical period for sexual imprinting in humans, analogous to critical periods in birds: "Rearing a person as a member of one sex rather than the other does not mean that there will be a difference in exposure to parents or other love objects; there will be, however, a difference in labeling of the self. Such labeling is perhaps irreversible because basic cognitive categorizations are irreversible" (p. 87). He then discussed Smedslund's (1961) work showing that while cognitive categorizations achieved before the age of cognitive constancies are easy to change, they are difficult to change after this age. But in this discussion Kohlberg overlooked the fact that Money and Hampson claimed that gender identity was difficult to change after the age of three, whereas Smedslund was talking about cognitive developmental steps normally taken at about the age of six. Kohlberg varied considerably with respect to which age or cognitive developmental level should be critical for children's achievement of gender constancy. As discussed later here, the range within which he varied (ages four to seven) is central to a developmental account of sex typing. However, the main import of Kohlberg's account is his placement of the acquisition of gender constancy at the same age as the shift to operational thought, at about five to seven years of age.

In the years following the publication of Kohlberg's 1966 paper, several writers became interested in the implications of gender constancy for imitation of same-sex models. This issue was important because social learning theorists were saying that imitation of same-sex models was a central process whereby children became sex-typed, whereas Kohlberg was arguing that the imitation of same-sex models was a consequence, rather than a cause, of the acquisition of gender schemas. He said that observational learning is "selective and internally organized by relational schemata" (Kohlberg, 1966, p. 83). With respect to the selective imitation of the same-sex parent, he argued that this should occur only after children had developed gender schemas that enabled them to know and value sex-appropriate activity. He thought that "effectance" or competence motivation would ensure that children would value the activities and characteristics appropriate for their own gender, once they understood what the gender-relevant attributes were. Kohlberg thought it was obvious that "a boy who desires to engage in masculine activities will prefer a male teacher or model to a female" (p. 127). Taking these two ideas together—that gender schemas only become firm organizing forces for behavior when gender constancy has been achieved, and that gender schemas provide the impetus for same-sex imitation—an obvious hypothesis was that such imitation should be more likely among children who were able to demonstrate gender constancy. It would also follow that same-sex imitation should not be common among children younger than the criterial age for gender constancy: somewhere between ages five and seven.

Maccoby and Jacklin (1974) reviewed the literature on imitation of same-sex models. In a series of studies in which children aged six or younger had been offered the opportunity to imitate either a single same-sex model or a single cross-sex model, the large majority of studies found no preferential imitation of the same-sex model. Over the age of six, there appeared to be an increased likelihood of same-sex imitation. These results seemed to fit nicely with the view that a child's motivation to seek out and utilize gender-appropriate information is enhanced by the achievement of gender constancy.

This view was also supported by other research. Ruble, Balaban, and Cooper (1981) found that children's utilization of information about the gender appropriateness of toys depended on their acquisition of gender constancy. In a study by Slaby and Frey (1975), with a group of children ranging in age from two to nearly six years, the children who had achieved gender constancy were more likely to selectively attend to same-sex models than were children who were not gender-constant. This was true even when chronological age had been controlled statistically. In this study, the measure used to reflect children's selective interest in same-sex models was the amount of time spent watching each of the two models. However, we know that observation of another person can reflect a variety of motives. It is worth noting that at low levels of gender constancy, girls actually spent somewhat more time watching male models than did boys, while at the higher levels the reverse was true. In the light of more recent work, the behavior of young girls might reflect wariness of, rather than identification with, males. In any case, the relationship of same-sex watching with gender constancy is the main point of interest.

Slaby and Frey (1975) raised an important point for subsequent work. They showed that the attainment of gender constancy is not an all-or-nothing phenomenon but rather a sequence of steps that form a Guttman scale. The ability to classify the self and others as to gender comes first, usually by age four. The next achievement is the understanding that one's gender is temporally stable: one always has been, and always will be, the same sex. And the final step is the understanding that gender is not affected by changes in hair style, clothing, or gender-typed activities. A boy can wear a dress or play with dolls and still be a boy. This last step, which Slaby and Frey call "gender consistency," follows fairly closely on the heels of temporal stability, both being achieved by the age of four-and-one-half years. This is surprisingly early. Emmerich and colleagues (Emmerich, Goldman, Kirsh, and Sharabany, 1977) found that among a large number of underprivileged children, the usual age for achieving gender constancy was considerably later, closer to age seven. Recent work by Wehren and DeLisi (1983) also pinpoints the age between five and seven years old as the usual time when children learn to maintain their gender designations in the face of changes in the gender appropriateness of a child's appearance or activities. They also found, however, that questions about temporal stability were answered correctly at an earlier age, commonly by age five. There is evidence that children's success in answering questions about gender constancy depends in part on the order and the way questions are asked (Siegal and Robinson, 1987) and whether pictorial aids or only verbal methods are used (Martin and Halverson, 1983). To the extent that the age of achieving gender constancy varies according to the aspect of constancy tested and the experimental procedure used, we are on slippery ground in trying to specify the age at which children should display a positive motivation to adopt behaviors appropriate to their sex.

The questions that Kohlberg and his supporters raised about the role of imitation in the acquisition of sex-typed behavior of young children soon drew a response from social learning theorists. In an elegantly designed study, Perry and Bussey (1979) exposed children to multiple models of both sexes. In one condition, four male models chose one activity, and four female models chose another. In another condition, the ratio of male-to-female choices of a given activity was three to one. In addition, there was a condition where equal numbers of male and female models chose an activity, and also a no-model control condition. In the first condition of high within-sex consensus among models, children consistently imitated the same-sex models. In the second condition of only moderate within-sex consensus, there was less same-sex imitation, but it was greater than chance. In the third condition of absence of model consensus, and in the no-model control condition, the children's activity choices were not sex-typed. In a second experiment, Perry and Bussey showed that children did not preferentially imitate a same-sex model if that model had previously been shown behaving sex-inappropriately. The authors concluded that imitation is alive and well as a process whereby sex-typed behavior is acquired, and they argued that social learning theory had been vindicated.

It is curious that Perry and Bussey's study was viewed as a refutation of cognitive developmental theory. First, the children who were subjects in the study were eight years old. Thus, they were old enough to easily fulfill the cognitive developmental requirement that children should have well-stabilized gender concepts and gender identity before they can be expected to imitate same-sex models selectively. Second, the fact that consensus among multiple models of the same sex fostered same-sex imitation indicates that children were forming abstractions or schemas on the basis of what they saw—abstractions concerning which behaviors are appropriate for males, which for females. To my knowledge, no cognitive developmental theorist has doubted that children learn a great deal about what activities are appropriate for the two sexes from observing male and female persons in real life and on television, and from reading about them in books. The issue has been whether, once aware of how people of a given sex behave, an observer will behave likewise. An observer who has many exemplars could learn a great deal about the distinctive behavior of the !Kung Bushmen without adopting the behavior. In short, the Perry and Bussey experiments left open the problem of an observer's motivation for imitating. This was the question that Kohlberg tried to answer through his emphasis on gender identity and sex constancy.

One could interpret the Perry and Bussey experiment as presenting a more serious challenge to psychoanalytic theory than to cognitive developmental theory. It indicated that children were unlikely to conclude from the behavior of a single model that the modeled behavior was relevant to sex typing. The child had to know that the model was a good exemplar of a gender class. This prerequisite has implications for the role of the same-sex parent as a prime source of sex typing. A girl who sees her mother both driving a car and wearing lipstick would not be able to tell which activity represents "feminine" behavior until she observes enough women and men to determine which behaviors distinguish the two sexes and which do not. The need for multiple models clearly called into question the idea that sex typing is based on identification with the same-sex parent.

A more serious challenge to cognitive developmental theory was presented by Bussey and Bandura (1984) in their study of a small group of privileged preschoolers ranging in age from twenty-nine to sixty-eight months. Once again multiple models were used, and in this study gender constancy was assessed. Subjects were selected so that there were equal numbers of subjects at each of three of Slaby and Frey's (1975) gender constancy levels. For both boys and girls, the mean number of imitative responses was nearly twice as great for the same-sex as for the cross-sex models. Both the amount of imitation and the levels of gender constancy increased with age, and age and gender constancy were highly correlated (.76 for boys, .82 for girls). Not surprisingly, when age was controlled statistically, gender constancy did not account for any additional variance in imitation. In this study, the number of subjects was small. In the model-exposed group, there were only three subjects of each sex at each of the three levels of gender constancy. Readers interested in the question of whether children who had not achieved any degree of gender constancy would selectively imitate must look for a significant difference in the choice of models between three very young girls and three very young boys. The data that would enable us to do this are not given in the published report, but the difference would have to be very large indeed to reach significance with these sample sizes. In a sample in which age and gender constancy are so heavily confounded, statistical controls will not succeed in pulling them apart. No doubt the authors could have just as easily reported that after controlling for gender constancy, there was no predictive power left for age.

The Bussey and Bandura study does provide clear evidence that children under the age of six will imitate same-sex models when multiple models are used and the actions that the models perform are perfectly correlated with their sex. As noted above, the test of the relevance of gender constancy is less clear. In their conclusion, the authors say that same-sex imitation "seems to involve relying on classifying males and females into distinct groups, recognizing personal similarity to one group of models, and tagging that group's behavior patterns in memory as the ones to be used as a guide to behavior" (1984, p. 1297). One can see here the evolution of social learning theory into cognitive social learning theory. The authors' conclusion is very much the same as what cognitive developmental theorists have been saying all along: imitation depends on the formation of gender schemas, and on the consonance of incoming information with an already formed gender identity. As other authors have noted (for example, Perry, White, and Perry, 1984), cognitive developmental theory and cognitive social learning theory no longer differ with respect to these elements in their accounts of sex typing. They both emphasize "self-socialization," to use the Maccoby and Jacklin (1974) term.

Gender Identity and Gender Cognition

What conditions did Bussey and Bandura think would lead an observer to "tag a behavior pattern in memory as a guide to behavior"? They believed they had demonstrated that gender constancy was not necessary. Citing Huston (1983), they say that "sex labeling and differential structuring of social experiences teach children to use the sex of the model as a guide for action" (1984, p. 1297). Based on evidence that children as young as six months of age can distinguish male from female faces, they imply that labeling must be a very early acquisition. However, discrimination and labeling are two different things: animals and infants can discriminate many things that they cannot label. Probably, accurate labeling of self and others as to gender is usually acquired toward the end of the third year. From this age on, gender identity takes on additional structure as children learn about the temporal stability of gender and its ability to survive changes in appearance and activities. Bussey and Bandura argue that simple labeling of self and other, along with some knowledge about the differential characteristics of the two sexes, is enough to motivate children to adopt sex-appropriate behavior. The issue seems to boil down to whether any greater coherence or stability of the gender self-concept, other than simple labeling, is needed for this motivation to be present and serve as a guide for children's behavior.

In thinking about this issue, we can glean insight into the nature of identity schemas from a recent study by Gelman, Collman, and Maccoby (1986). This study dealt with gender inferences. Preschool-age children were asked questions about a series of picture sets such as presented in Figure 1. For each set, children were given either familiar or unfamiliar information about the boy and girl pictured on the top row. For example, for one set, the experimenter said, pointing to the boy, "this boy has little seeds inside"; then, pointing to the girl, "this girl has little eggs inside." Next, pointing to the third child (dressed like the girl above), the experimenter asked one of two different questions: (1) "This child has seeds inside. Is this a boy or a girl?" or (2) "This child is a boy. Does he have seeds or eggs inside?" Questions of the second kind were much easier for the children to understand and were usually answered correctly by four-year-olds. The same children did not do better than chance on the first question. In other words, young children easily made inferences about gender properties once they were told the core gender category to which someone belonged; they could not make the reverse inference, however, from property to category.

In this same study, the children were given a standard gender constancy test. Their performance on these questions was at a chance level. It can be seen that most of the items on measures of gender constancy

Figure 1. Sample Picture Set Used in the Classification, Property Inference, and Control Conditions

require an inference from property to category. Children are asked, "if this boy wears a dress, or does girl things, is he a boy or a girl?" Those of preschool age usually cannot answer correctly, even though they know full well that if the boy were a boy, he would not wear a dress or do "girl things."

These findings can be put into the context of some recent work on identity constancy in natural kinds (Gelman and Markman, 1987; Keil, 1986). Keil presented young children with a task very similar to the species constancy problem used by Kohlberg (1966) and DeVries (1969). Starting with a picture of a racoon, Keil showed its hair being cut short, a stripe being painted down its back, and a little bag of smelly material being placed under its tail, so that it looked and smelled like a skunk. The question was whether the animal was still a racoon. Did it still have racoon blood? Would it have racoon babies or skunk babies? Alternatively, children were presented with changes in an artifact: a pitcher being transformed into a vase by having its spout and handle taken away. Many children preserved the identity of the racoon while readily agreeing that the pitcher had been changed into a vase. The claim is that there are certain kinds of categories that have a core identity from which children readily induce hidden properties. Younger children may not know what defining characteristics an adult would use to classify an exemplar into a category, but, nevertheless, once they have decided that an exemplar *is* a member of a natural-kind category, children as young as age three will readily infer that it has additional hidden properties. Children make inferences on the basis of category membership that they are unwilling to make on the basis of perceptual similarity.

The relevance of this work for issues of gender identity seems to be as follows. The categories male and female are natural kinds. That is, they are rather like species categories and unlike artifacts such as pitchers. Children are likely to entertain wide-ranging, deep theories about the properties male or female creatures might have. Once children are either provided with a gender label or else produce the label themselves on the basis of a person's name, appearance, or activities, the label becomes a basis for attributing to that person a whole cluster of characteristics associated with gender. The label becomes a kind of magnet, attracting new information about gender characteristics. As Hough, Hoffman, and Cowan (1980) have shown, if three-year-olds are told that a given child is a boy, they will claim that the child is smart, big, strong, mad, fast, loud, and mean; and if that child is a girl, they will claim that the child is dumb, weak, soft, little, scared, slow, quiet, and nice. The research cited above suggests that children make such inferences from a natural-kind category such as gender, while they are unlikely to do so for other categories or artifacts.

Stereotypes around natural-kind categories form quickly and early. This does not mean, however, that a young child understands the defining criteria for placing an exemplar in the category. Just as young children may not know that an island is defined as a body of land entirely surrounded by water, rather than as a body of land with palm trees or beaches, they may not know that human gender is defined by primary and secondary sex characteristics. Even if they are aware of the defining attributes at an early age, their selection of and reliance on these attributes as crucial for categorization comes considerably later. The switch to utilization of defining attributes does not come all at once; it is domain specific. Hence we cannot point to a specific age at which children should come to base their gender judgments on adultlike criteria. No doubt this development varies from child to child, depending in part on the information available to each child. It may be that the switch to a reliance on defining attributes makes a child less vulnerable to a belief that people's gender can change, if the defining attributes are themselves stable. Yet clearly children can believe their gender is stable without knowing its defining attributes.

We know that children who are too young to pass the usual gender constancy test nevertheless display clear sex typing in their behavior. The Bussey and Bandura experiment discussed earlier indicates that if the information about gender is made clear through convergent information from multiple models, children will imitate same-sex others at a young age—younger than the age at which we might expect them to understand the consistency of gender through a series of transformations. Do these facts mean that Kohlberg was wrong and that a firm, stable gender identity is not needed for sex typing to occur? Or does it mean that Kohlberg was right about the importance of the gender self-schema for sex typing, but children develop a firm, stable gender identity earlier than Kohlberg thought?

There is good reason to favor the latter view. It is instructive to consider a phenomenon observed by Marcus and Overton (1978) when they contrasted a pictorial version of the gender constancy test with one in which live children were used as models. A classmate of the subject stood behind a wooden frame so that overlays could be used to change the child's hairstyle and clothing. Marcus and Overton noted that in the live-model condition their subjects became acutely uncomfortable as they observed these changes, so much so that their performance was disrupted. The children's discomfort appears to reflect a strong conviction that such changes really could not and should not be occurring. Marcus and Overton also found that nearly all of their youngest subjects (kindergarten age) said that they and other children could not change their gender if they wanted to. In other words, they really believed that their gender was constant, even though they failed other gender constancy tests.

Appearance-reality distinctions are important in this domain of questioning, and Trautner (1985) reports that children who have difficulty making appearance-reality distinctions are also likely to be confused on the gender constancy questions. In other words, when asked whether gender changes when a child wears cross-gender clothes or hairstyles, some children may not be sure whether the experimenter is asking whether the child has *really* changed sex or only appears to have done so. Some of the gender constancy questions appear to invite children to adopt a playful or phantasizing judgmental set. As Martin and Halverson (1983) have shown, children who adopt a "pretend" set are more likely to fail gender constancy items. Siegal and Robinson (1987) report that four-year-olds, when told about another child who said that a little girl would become a boy if she played boys' games, frequently explain the other child's answer in ways that indicate they are just pretending in order to please the experimenter.

It seems clear that Kohlberg, and some of the rest of us, were misled by the gender constancy test. As the study by Gelman and colleagues shows, this test calls for a kind of inference that is difficult for young children to make. Furthermore, it appears to require that children adopt a small set of defining attributes for gender and avoid taking a pretend rather than a reality judgmental set. These modes are often not characteristic of the way young children categorize. A four-year-old's failure to pass the test probably does not mean that the child lacks a firm, stable gender identity, or even that the child is often in doubt about the gender of other persons. Gender is one of the most overdetermined elements of identity. We use gender-specific personal pronouns and proper names. To these we add indicators in the way of clothing and hairstyles. It may be, too, that such culturally specific indicators are merged with more universally available cues to gender. Whatever the cluster of cues children use, the point is that it would be very difficult for a child to be in doubt about his or her gender after the age of three or four, or to believe that one's gender is really subject to change.

Does this mean that gender concepts are not, after all, connected to general cognitive growth? Not at all. The hundreds of studies of conservation conducted after Piaget's original work have indicated that the achievement of conservation is not an all-or-nothing structural change, and that aspects of conservation are available much earlier than Piaget thought, if assessment methods are appropriately geared to children's productive capacities. Thus, the achievement of gender constancy at age four would not be out of synchrony with early levels of constancy in other domains.

In short, one could take the position that none of the research done in the years since the publication of Kohlberg's 1966 paper invalidates the idea that a firm and stable gender identity schema is a necessary condition for motivating children to match their own behavior to what they understand to be sex-appropriate characteristics. The existing research does not definitively *validate* the Kohlbergian hypothesis either. The important questions simply remain open. And we should be aware that even if Kohlberg was right about the motivation that underlies self-socialization for sex typing, it would still be possible for some degree of early sex-differentiation (that is, any occurring in the first two or three years of life) to be present as a result of factors other than gender identity schemas—factors such as biologically prepared behavior patterns that differ by sex, or early differential conditioning.

The above analysis suggests that the essential elements of gender constancy are usually in place by about age four. Furthermore, this stable self-concept can be present, and can motivate children's adoption of sex-typed behavior, even though at this age children do not understand the defining attributes of gender. The question of defining attributes is an important one, and one that Kohlberg struggled with. He cited an example of a boy, just turning six years of age, who when he saw his father carrying his mother's purse said, "Why are you carrying the purse, dad?

Are you a lady or something? You must be a lady; men don't carry purses" (Kohlberg, 1966, p. 116). Kohlberg suggested that children have a strong need to maintain their gender identity: "Until the child, at around age seven, establishes an abstract, constant definition of gender based on anatomy, his gender self-categorization is related to every possible sex-typed attribute" (1966, p. 116). He thought that this condition was temporary, however, and that with increasing anatomical knowledge children would become "more discriminating and less compulsive" in their use of sex-typed traits for making judgments about gender identity.

Gender Flexibility

Kohlberg appears to have enunciated two rather incompatible principles. On the one hand, there was the claim we have been discussing: once children know that their sex is a stable personal attribute, then they will value sex-appropriate activities and will become especially interested in same-sex others because of their similarity to the self. In particular, the child will begin to take the same-sex parent, and presumably other same-sex persons, as preferred models and will become more strongly tied emotionally to same-sex others. Thus, processes are set in motion by the achievement of gender constancy, which strengthens sex typing. Kohlberg's countervailing theme, on the other hand, was that the achievement of gender constancy makes sex typing more flexible (weaker?). Children who know that their gender identity will not change no longer need to worry about conforming to all the attributes of their gender for fear of changing into the other sex.

Kohlberg's hypothesis about gender flexibility has been strongly revived in more recent writings. Huston (1983, p. 407) says, "a full understanding of gender constancy marks a turning point that permits (but does not guarantee) a decrease in rigidity and an increase in flexibility of children's concepts about sex-typing." Serbin and Sprafkin (1986) studied children at each year of age between three and seven and found that while gender knowledge was increasing sharply during this time, and affiliation toward same-sex others also increased, gender salience diminished. Children in this study were asked to group pictures of people according to which seemed to go together; gender was a possible basis, but the pictures could also be classified on the basis of the activities in which the pictured people were engaged. Young children most often classified by gender, older children by activity. Of course, from this finding we do not know whether gender had become less salient or activity more so as children approached age seven.

A decrease in gender salience at about age six or seven is certainly a possible explanation for the Serbin and Sprafkin results. However, it is difficult to believe that gender is not salient for six- and seven-year-olds, or that their gender concepts are flexible, even for those who do have a stable gender identity. We may recall Damon's (1977) interviews with children from age four to age ten, in which he found that children aged six and seven were intensely sexist; for example, they believed that it was morally wrong for a boy to wear a dress. Older children were more flexible, in that they believed such a boy might be stupid but not naughty. In a review of work on gender segregation and related phenomena, Maccoby (1988) reports that gender segregation is powerfully maintained by children, even (perhaps especially) in the absence of adult pressure, up to at least age ten.

I suggest that the achievement of gender constancy does not make children more flexible with respect to sex typing. Gender constancy has to do with identity judgments, not with the stereotypes that surround a gender category once an identity judgment is made. A boy of seven or eight years of age may know that he will not turn into a girl if he carries his mother's purse. Nevertheless, he would be acutely embarrassed if another boy saw him doing so and would avoid such an action. After children understand about the temporal stability of their gender, all the powerful forces for adopting sex-typed behavior that Kohlberg pointed to—affiliation with same-sex others, the need for cognitive and personal consistency, and so on—are still in place and still motivate children to adopt sex-typed behavior and attitudes. If children become more flexible in some respects by, say, age nine or ten, I argue that this has nothing to do with gender constancy, which we now believe is achieved much earlier (at around age four). Rather, the flexibility probably reflects increasing information about how tight the connection is between gender and a range of activities. For most activities, there is not complete model consensus, and children amass information about exceptions as they grow older. They learn which inferences from category membership can be widely generalized and which cannot. In the experiment by Gelman, Collman, and Maccoby (1986), four-year-olds appeared ready to make a very wide range of inferences about a child once they knew the child's sex. Given that a child was a boy, they were ready to believe that he had seeds rather than eggs inside, that he had andro rather than estro in his blood, and so on. Older children, with their greater knowledge about exceptions, might not be so willing to make such broad inferences about unfamiliar qualities; certainly, they would hesitate to make inferences that ran contrary to generalizations based on their own prior knowledge.

Sex-role flexibility grows in another way that again may have nothing to do with gender constancy. Children learn to discriminate among situations in terms of how relevant gender is to each situation. Gender will always be relevant, and hence salient, when people are dating or otherwise involved in mate selection. Gender is more relevant on the school playground than in the classroom, at least in coeducational schools. Gender schemas are always available, but as several writers have noted (for example, Deaux and Major, 1987; Bem, 1981) they are not always called into play. Kohlberg would probably have thought of gender as so central a part of self-identity that we never divest ourselves of it nor function with gender in abeyance. Recent thinkers about gender salience imply that we can and do function without regard to gender under some circumstances. The central question is what are the conditions that determine when and whether our gender schemas will be activated? Current issues, then, take us away from the ground Kohlberg charted. Nevertheless, our thinking about gender can never be the same as it would have been had Kohlberg not written about it.

References

Bem, S. L. "Gender Schema Theory: A Cognitive Account of Sex-Typing." *Psychological Review*, 1981, *88*, 354–364.

Bussey, K., and Bandura, A. "Influence of Gender Constancy and Social Power on Sex-Linked Modeling." *Journal of Personality and Social Psychology*, 1984, *47*, 1292–1302.

Damon, W. M. *The Social World of the Child*. San Francisco: Jossey-Bass, 1977.

Deaux, K., and Major, B. "Putting Gender into Context: An Interactive Model of Gender-Related Behavior." *Psychological Review*, 1987, *94*, 369–389.

DeLucia, L. A. "The Toy Preference Test: A Measure of Sex-Role Identification." *Child Development*, 1963, *34*, 107–117.

DeVries, R. "Constancy of Generic Identity in the Years Three to Six." *Monographs of the Society for Research in Child Development*, 1969, *34*. (Serial no. 127.)

Emmerich, W., Goldman, K. S., Kirsh, B., and Sharabany, R. "Evidence for a Transitional Phase in the Development of Gender Constancy." *Child Development*, 1977, *48*, 930–936.

Fagot, B. I. "Beyond the Reinforcement Principle: Another Step Toward Understanding Sex Roles." *Developmental Psychology*, 1985, *21*, 1097–1104.

Gelman, S. A., Collman, P., and Maccoby, E. E. "Inferring Properties from Categories Versus Inferring Categories from Properties: The Case of Gender." *Child Development*, 1986, *57*, 396–404.

Gelman, S. A., and Markman, E. "Young Children's Inductions from Natural Kinds: The Role of Categories and Appearances." *Child Development*, 1987, *58*, 1532–1541.

Haugh, S. S., Hoffman, C. D., and Cowan, G. "The Age of the Very Young Beholder: Sex Typing of Infants by Very Young Children." *Child Development*, 1980, *51*, 598–600.

Huston, A. "Sex Typing." In P. H. Mussen (ed.), *Handbook of Child Psychology*. (4th ed.) Vol. 4. New York: Wiley, 1983.

Keil, F. C. "The Acquisition of Natural Kinds and Artifact Terms." In W. Demopoulos and A. Marras (eds.), *Language Learning and Concept Acquisition*. Norwood, N.J.: Ablex, 1986.

Kohlberg, L. "A Cognitive-Developmental Analysis of Children's Sex-Role Concepts and Attitudes." In E. E. Maccoby (ed.), *The Development of Sex Differences*. Stanford, Calif.: Stanford University Press, 1966.

Maccoby, E. E. "Gender as a Social Category." *Developmental Psychology*, 1988, *24*, 755-765.

Maccoby, E. E., and Jacklin, C. N. *The Psychology of Sex Differences*. Stanford, Calif.: Stanford University Press, 1974.

Marcus, D. E., and Overton, W. F. "The Development of Cognitive Gender Constancy and Sex-Role Preferences." *Child Development*, 1978, *49*, 434-444.

Martin, C. L., and Halverson, C. F., Jr. "Gender Constancy: A Methodological and Theoretical Analysis." *Sex Roles*, 1983, *9*, 775-790.

Money, J., Hampson, J. G., and Hampson, J. L. "Imprinting and the Establishment of Gender Role." *Archives of Neurological Psychiatry*, 1957, *77*, 333-336.

Perry, D. G., and Bussey, K. "The Social Learning Theory of Sex Differences: Initiation Is Alive and Well." *Journal of Personality and Social Psychology*, 1979, *37*, 1699-1712.

Perry, D. G., White, A. V., and Perry, L. C. "Is Early Sex-Typing Due to Children's Attempts to Match Their Behavior to Sex-Role Stereotypes?" *Child Development*, 1984, *55*, 2114-2121.

Ruble, D. N., Balaban, T., and Cooper, J. "Gender Constancy and the Effects of Sex-Typed Televised Toy Commercials." *Child Development*, 1981, *52*, 667-673.

Serbin, L. A., and Sprafkin, C. "The Salience of Gender and the Process of Sex Typing in Three- to Seven-Year-Old Children." *Child Development*, 1986, *57*, 1188-1199.

Siegal, M., and Robinson, J. "Order Effects in Children's Gender-Constancy Responses." *Developmental Psychology*, *23* (2), 283-286.

Slaby, R. G., and Frey, K. S. "Development of Gender Constancy and Selective Attribution to Same-Sex Models." *Child Development*, 1975, *46*, 849-856.

Smedslund, J. "The Acquisition of Conservation of Substance and Weight in Children. III: Extinction of Conservation of Weight Acquired Normally and by Means of Empirical Controls on a Balance." *Scandinavian Journal of Psychology*, 1961, *2*, 1-3.

Trautner, H. M. "The Significance of the Appearance-Reality Distinction for the Development of Gender Constancy." Paper presented at the biennial meeting of the Society for Research in Child Development, Toronto, Ontario, Canada, April 1985.

Wehren, A., and DeLisi, R. "The Development of Gender Understanding: Judgments and Explanations." *Child Development*, 1983, *54*, 1568-1578.

Eleanor E. Maccoby is emeritus professor of psychology, Stanford University. She is the author of numerous articles and several books, including Social Development: Psychological Growth and the Parent-Child Relationship *(1980) and, with Carol Jacklin,* The Psychology of Sex Differences *(1974).*

The gender concept category system traces its roots to Kohlberg's legacy and serves as a prototype for all social category systems.

The Gender Concept Development Legacy

Ronald G. Slaby

As an anonymous philosopher once said, "There are only two types of people in this world—those who divide people into two types and those who do not."

Lawrence Kohlberg was the first to convince us that, our anonymous philosopher notwithstanding, there is really only one type of person in this world: the person who invariably develops from one who does not divide people into two types to one who does. He convinced most of us that the gender concept represents a developing cognitive system for categorizing all individuals, including oneself, as male or female; for connecting a wide variety of attributes to the categories; and for organizing and regulating one's social functioning.

I am honored to have the opportunity to comment on Eleanor Maccoby's review of Lawrence Kohlberg's formulations of gender concept development. The work of these two individuals inspired me more than fifteen years ago to begin looking for interconnections and new formulations that might unite certain essential features of the social learning and the cognitive developmental paradigms into a new research paradigm. Although the task continues, Maccoby's chapter in this volume illustrates that initial success is evident in generating a new social-cognitive development paradigm that reaches far beyond the area of sex-role development.

Kohlberg's Formulation of the Gender Concept

The growth of the two main theoretical traditions that guided the last quarter century of research on sex-role development is described by Huston

(1983) in a visually rich metaphor: Like trees growing on opposite sides of a road, the social learning theory and the cognitive developmental theory have grown closer over time—their branches reaching across the road to meet and even intertwine, while their roots remain separated by the road. I would add that a new growth of saplings has occurred, generated from the seeds of the parent trees and promising to express in a new form the essence of both parents. The social-cognitive development paradigm promises to carry Lawrence Kohlberg's legacy forward into the next generation.

In his extraordinary 1966 paper, Kohlberg's formulation of gender concept development was an act of scientific revolution. As Maccoby points out, it is a sign of the success of this revolution that, in hindsight, many aspects of his revolutionary formulations seem obvious to us today. While many of his assertions have already been widely adopted and built on, others continue to provoke researchers because they seem controversial, unsubstantiated, or even misleading. It is noteworthy that whether Kohlberg's assertions are now considered "right" or "wrong," they are impossible to disregard.

Perhaps the most remarkable aspect of Kohlberg's 1966 paper was that he chose to bring the cognitive developmental approach to the topic of sex-role development. Unlike the area of moral development, where Kohlberg looked to Piaget's work as a basis for further exploration and formulation, the area of sex-role development was an uncharted and theoretically hostile territory for a cognitive developmentalist to enter, particularly since it required an explanation of differential behavior from a theory that claimed universal stages in cognitive development. Kohlberg entered a territory held by Freudian and social learning theorists and recharted this territory in cognitive developmental terms, altering forever the path of research in this field. Kohlberg continued to ponder many aspects of his gender concept formulation in light of the twenty years of research since his original 1958 paper, as evidenced by a series of meetings that he and I held on this topic in 1986. He pointed out that in the mid-1960s the topic of sex-role development was considered the least likely arena for a cognitive developmentalist to enter. In this sense, Kohlberg's paper represented a theoretical coup that took other theorists by complete surprise.

Many aspects of Kohlberg's original formulation have evolved into issues of current interest in the field. Maccoby brought insight and clarity to a number of them, and I here supplement Maccoby's discussion by addressing the following issues: (1) the characteristics of the gender category system; (2) the role of the gender category system in self-socialization; and (3) sex role flexibility and the perceived link between gender category and attributes.

Gender Category Characteristics

The particular characteristics of a given category system may play an important role in determining the way in which attributes are linked to the categories as well as the way in which social functioning is organized and regulated. As Maccoby (1988) pointed out, once a social category system has been established cognitively, it can become a powerful organizer of social functioning. Although the gender concept serves as only one of many social category systems that individuals use to organize and regulate their social functioning, in many ways the gender category system is broadly regarded by all peoples of the world to possess the following characteristics:

1. Mutually exclusive (one cannot be both male and female)
2. Exhaustive (one cannot be neither male nor female)
3. Inclusive of oneself (in contrast to category systems that permit exemption of oneself)
4. Binary (a two-category system)
5. Absolute (one cannot be degrees of male or female, although one can be degrees of "masculine" and "feminine")
6. Equally distributive (dividing people approximately 50-50 percent)
7. Easily perceivable (multiple, easily perceivable markers generally exist to enable gender categorization)
8. Stable (one's gender is invariant over time)
9. Consistent (one's gender is invariant across situations and personal motivations)
10. Unchangeable (one's gender cannot be altered, disregarding exceptions, for the moment)
11. Based on natural kind categories (derived from naturally occurring biological variation)
12. Biologically complementary (both are needed to perpetuate the species)
13. Regarded as broadly predictive (to varying degrees, treated in all societies as predictive of a variety of attributes that exceed the essential defining properties of gender, often including attitudes, behaviors, cognitions, emotions, motivations, propensities, temperaments, and values).

Since individuals in all societies develop an understanding and acceptance of these relatively content-free and structural characteristics of the gender category system, they can be considered universal. However, wide cultural variation in the specific content and range of the attributes linked to the categories of male and female can be expected, as Mead (1935) has described.

Cultural variation in the emphasis of various characteristics might also be expected. For example, the American term "the opposite sex" emphasizes the mutual exclusivity feature, while de-emphasizing the biological complementarity feature. I am told by my Asian colleagues that this term seems foreign and strange to them given the essential complementary nature of man and woman. Recent research evidence suggests that young children typically develop a mutual exclusivity bias in their word learning that has implications for their concept development (Merriman and Bowman, 1988). Indeed, before the mid 1970s, when Bem developed the concept of androgyny, together with an instrument for measuring masculinity and femininity independently of each other, American psychologists regularly built the mutual exclusivity characteristic of the gender category into scales of masculinity–femininity. In so doing, they predefined as polar opposites those attributes that are generally regarded in our culture as linked in some way to the gender categories.

Additionally, the characteristics measured in the most often used gender constancy scales developed in the 1970s (Emmerich, Goldman, Kirsch, and Sharabany, 1977; Slaby and Frey, 1975) were designed to address only a specific subset of the characteristics of the gender category system. Other measures such as genital knowledge, emphasized by Freud and measured by both Bem (1989) and McConaghy (1979), may tap other characteristics of the developing gender category system. Each characteristic has its own particular implications for the way in which the gender category system organizes and regulates social functioning.

The gender category system shares many characteristics with other broad social category systems, such as race, ethnicity, nationality, and age. Yet, by virtue of its unique combination of characteristics, it serves as a prototype for other social category systems. Much can be learned by comparing and contrasting the characteristics and the influences of other social category systems with those of gender (for example, Aboud, 1988; Carey, 1985; Fisher and Elmendorf, 1986; Slaby and Quarfoth, 1983).

The Gender Category System and Self-Socialization

One of Kohlberg's most controversial claims was that children's developing gender identity schemas (as distinct from their understanding of attributes linked to the categories of male and female) play an active role in organizing and regulating their social functioning. Reversing the social learning position of the time, Kohlberg (1966, p. 89) wrote that "The social learning syllogism is: 'I want rewards, I am rewarded for doing boy things, therefore I want to be a boy.' In contrast, a cognitive theory assumes this sequence: 'I am a boy, therefore, I want to do boy things, therefore the opportunity to do boy things (and to gain approval for doing them) is rewarding.'"

Subsequent research demonstrates that the organizing and regulating role of the developing gender category system takes many forms, including selective attention to same-sex models (Slaby and Frey, 1975); selective avoidance of activities performed by different-sex models; evaluation that a toy played with by different-sex models is inappropriate for same-sex individuals (Ruble, Balaban, and Cooper, 1981); selective susceptibility to reinforcement by same-sex individuals (Fagot, 1985); and a variety of sex-typed preferences (for example, Kuhn, Nash, and Brucken, 1978; Martin and Little, 1987; Smetana and Letourneau, 1984).

Constantinople (1979) characterized this form of cognitive organization and regulation as top-down, concept-driven processing, in contrast to bottom-up, data-driven processing. Bem (1981) and Martin and Halverson (1981) characterized this phenomenon in terms of gender schematic processing.

Although primary emphasis in these accounts rests on the way in which the gender category system serves as an organizer of data input, the gender category system may also serve as an active agent of "self-socialization." Maccoby and Jacklin (1974) generated this term to describe Kohlberg's notion of the active role played by the developing gender category system in regulating an individual's socialization experiences and social behaviors. According to this notion, a child uses his or her gender category system not merely as a passive organizer of data input but also as a way to actively seek out social information (often simple, incomplete, or even distorted). From this data the child induces organized rules regarding what is sex-appropriate and makes inferences beyond the data given. Despite that these child-induced rules are often oversimplified, exaggerated, stereotyped, or based on outright distortions of reality, the child nevertheless actively attempts to fit his or her own behavior to these rules.

The concept of self-socialization deserves further development and use in the area of sex-role research and beyond (Slaby, 1980). For example, Aboud (1988) and Triviz (1987) have begun to examine the relationship of both ethnic and gender identity development to children's stereotyping and selective social behavior. The key conceptual components in need of further development and investigation of their relationships seem to be the following: (1) a developing social category system, (2) cognitive inductions and inferences based on active selection, organization, and linkage of various attributes to the social categories, and (3) social behavior.

It appears that social categories play a particularly important and potentially dominating role in human cognition and cognitively mediated social behavior. Once a social category is established, individuals may be ready to make category-linked inferences beyond the data given and to regulate their own behavior in accordance with these inferences.

The Gender Category System and Sex-Role Flexibility

If the child invariably becomes a person who divides the world into two types, what permits this developing individual to achieve a measure of freedom from the potential dominance or tyranny of the gender category system? Maccoby (this volume) and Deaux and Major (1987) suggest that we investigate the issue of sex-role flexibility by examining the particular conditions under which the gender category system is called into play. I further suggest, in accordance with Kohlberg's formulations, that the question of sex-role flexibility involves the development of an individual's understanding of the nature of the links between gender category and associated attributes, as well as the development of an individual's cognitive ability to reflect on his or her own thought processes regarding these links. The link between gender category and a given attribute can be described as one of the following:

1. Necessity (that defines and dictates an absolute dominance of category over attribute)
2. Propensity (that suggests that inherent influence of category over attribute)
3. Societal probability (that personally accepts a societal norm of perceived association between category and attribute)
4. Self-generated probability (that acknowledges that one's own perceived association between category and attribute may differ from that of societal norms)
5. Self-generated disengagement (that personally chooses to disregard societal norms as invalid, irrelevant, or unjust, while recognizing that other individuals may not do so).

Although these alternatives are not necessarily mutually exclusive, this sequence of alternatives may represent steps in the development of sex-role flexibility. Ultimate sex-role flexibility may involve an understanding and a mastery of the selective use of alternatives such as these in guiding one's own social functioning as well as in understanding the concepts and behaviors of others.

To briefly illustrate this idea, consider the following situation. You are asked to go to the airport to meet Dr. Smith, a medical doctor. You arrive as the one hundred adult passengers (fifty men and fifty women) are leaving the plane. Your only means to identify Dr. Smith is to ask individual passengers their names. Since you have only enough time to ask ten passengers, you risk missing Dr. Smith.

If you are a young child without an established gender category system, you may randomly choose ten passengers without regard to gender, thereby choosing, on average, five men and five women. But if you are a young child who has developed a gender category system, as well as a perceived link of necessity between the male category and the doctor occupation, you may use the 100 percent rule, thereby choosing ten men. It is noteworthy that given even a slightly disproportionate favoring of males as doctors in our society, use of the 100 percent rule represents a maximizing strategy for successful identification of Dr. Smith. At the same time, the perceived link of necessity between category and attribute represents the most extreme form of stereotyping.

If you are a somewhat more cognitively advanced child, you may no longer perceive the link between male and doctor to be definitional and absolute but rather to be one of propensity (based on a notion that men are inherently better suited than women to become doctors). In this case, you might also choose ten men, but you would not be closed to the possibility of choosing a woman under exceptional circumstances, such as seeing a woman wearing a stethoscope.

If you consider the possibility of the link between male and doctor to be one of societal probability rather than of necessity or propensity, you may use social norms to guide your choices. Thus, you may choose eight men, based on a perceived norm that eight times out of ten a doctor will be a man.

If you have achieved some independence from societal norms, you may generate your own probability of the link between male and doctor. Your choices may vary considerably from those of others, depending on your own data and your cognitive system for organizing that data. Yet, even in a data-sensitive system in which choices are guided by self-generated probabilities, the gender category system can be expected to play a major role in selectively perceiving and organizing the data.

If you perceive the link between male and doctor to be irrelevant, or recognize that social injustices may be perpetuated by presuming such a link, you may adopt a strategy of attempting to disregard gender in making your choices of passengers to ask. Yet, the gender category system may be so central to your social functioning that particular forms of active cognitive monitoring of your own thought process may be needed to disengage its influence.

In our social world, total disengagement of our gender category system, once it has been established, is probably neither possible nor adaptive. Indeed, initial investigation of the perceived mutability of the link between gender categories and attributes of adults has revealed interesting sex differences and individual differences worthy of further investigation (Schelhas-Miller, 1988). Yet through a form of cognitive mastery over alternative uses of one's own cognitive category system, considerable sex-role flexibility can theoretically be achieved. In this sense, Kohlberg's one type of person, who invariably develops from one who does not divide people into two types to one who does, might further develop into a person who achieves some cognitive control over the uses and implications of the dividing process.

In his formulation of gender concept development, Kohlberg has indeed left us with a rich legacy from which to develop further not only our theories but also ourselves.

References

Aboud, F. *Children and Prejudice*. New York: Blackwell, 1988.
Bem, S. L. "The Measurement of Psychological Androgyny." *Journal of Consulting and Clinical Psychology*, 1974, *42*, 155-162.
Bem, S. L. "Gender Schema Theory: A Cognitive Account of Sex-Typing." *Psychological Review*, 1981, *88*, 354-364.
Bem, S. L. "Genital Knowledge and Gender Constancy in Preschool Children." *Child Development*, 1989, *60*, 649-662.
Carey, S. *Conceptual Change in Childhood*. Cambridge, Mass.: MIT Press, 1985.
Constantinople, A. "Sex-Role Acquisition: In Search of the Elephant." *Sex Roles*, 1979, *5*, 121-133.
Deaux, K., and Major, B. "Putting Gender into Context: An Interactive Model of Gender-Related Behavior." *Psychological Review*, 1987, *94*, 369-389.
Emmerich, W., Goldman, K. S., Kirsh, B., and Sharabany, R. "Evidence for a Transitional Phase in the Development of Gender Constancy." *Child Development*, 1977, *48*, 930-936.
Fagot, B. I. "Beyond the Reinforcement Principle: Another Step Toward Understanding Sex Roles." *Developmental Psychology*, 1985, *21*, 1097-1104.
Fisher, K. W., and Elmendorf, D. M. "Becoming a Different Person: Transformations in Personality and Social Behavior." In M. Perlmutter (ed.), *Cognitive Perspectives on Children's Social Development. The Minnesota Symposia on Child Psychology*. Hillsdale, N.J.: Erlbaum, 1986.
Huston, A. "Sex Typing." In P. H. Mussen (ed.), *Handbook of Child Psychology*. (4th ed.) Vol. 4. New York: Wiley, 1983.
Kohlberg, L. "A Cognitive-Developmental Analysis of Children's Sex-Role Concepts and Attitudes." In E. E. Maccoby (ed.), *The Development of Sex Differences*. Stanford, Calif.: Stanford University Press, 1966.
Kuhn, D., Nash, S. C., and Brucken, L. "Sex Role Concepts of Two- and Three-Year Olds." *Child Development*, 1978, *49*, 445-451.
Maccoby, E. E. "Gender as a Social Category." *Developmental Psychology*, 1988, *24*, 755-765.
Maccoby, E. E., and Jacklin, C. N. *The Psychology of Sex Differences*. Stanford, Calif.: Stanford University Press, 1974.
McConaghy, M. J. "Gender Permanence and the Genital Basis of Gender: Stages in the Development of Constancy of Gender Identity." *Child Development*, 1979, *50*, 1223-1226.
Martin, C. L., and Halverson, O. F. "A Schematic Processing Model of Sex Typing and Stereotyping in Children." *Child Development*, 1981, *52*, 1119-1134.
Martin, C. L., and Little, J. K. "The Influence of Gender Understanding on Children's Sex-Typed Preferences and Gender Stereotypes." Unpublished manuscript, University of British Columbia, Vancouver, Canada, 1987.

Mead, M. *Sex and Temperament.* New York: Morrow, 1935.

Merriman, W. E., and Bowman, L. L. "The Mutual Exclusivity Bias in Children's Word Learning." *Monographs for the Society for Research in Child Development,* 1988, *54* (3-4). (Serial no. 220.)

Ruble, D., Balaban, T., and Cooper, J. "Gender Constancy and the Effect of Televised Toy Commercials." *Child Development,* 1981, *52,* 667-673.

Schelhas-Miller, C. "The Perceived Mutability of Gender-Linked Attributes." Doctoral dissertation, Harvard University, 1988.

Slaby, R. G. "The Self-Socialization of Boys and Girls: How Children's Developing Concept of Gender Influences Their Sex-Role Behavior." In J. M. Samson (ed.), *Enfancé et sexualité* [Childhood and sexuality]. Montreal: Editions Études Vivantes, 1980.

Slaby, R. G., and Frey, K. S. "Development of Gender Constancy and Selective Attention to Same-Sex Models." *Child Development,* 1975, *46,* 849-856.

Slaby, R. G., and Quarfoth, G. R. "Children's Perceptions of Age and Sex Similarity as Determinant of Selective Social Learning." Paper presented at the biennial meeting of the Society for Research in Child Development, Detroit, Michigan, April 1983.

Smetana, J. G., and Letourneau, K. J. "Development of Gender Constancy and Children's Sex-Typed Free Play Behavior." *Developmental Psychology,* 1984, *20,* 691-695.

Triviz, R. M. "Gender's Salience over Ethnicity in First Graders' Identifications." Doctoral dissertation, Harvard University, 1987.

Ronald G. Slaby is senior scientist, Education Development Center, and lecturer on pediatrics, Harvard University Medical School. He currently develops educational programs that focus on preventing violence in schools and is a consultant for public television presentations such as "Private Violence/Public Crisis."

The major emphasis of Kohlberg's research was on moral judgments, but moral action was an essential component of his research and theory.

Moral Judgment, Action, and Development

Elliot Turiel

The study of relationships between moral judgments and action is itself a problem of attempting to coordinate several complex variables in an intricate fashion. As with most problems that entail coordinating variables, it is often necessary to deeply analyze each variable separately, as well as to examine their intersection. In several researchers' long-term efforts at understanding social and moral development, we see varying, and sometimes oscillating, patterns of concentration on judgment, action, or their coordination. This process of analysis involves a continuously shifting pattern of concentration on the variables that was always at the core of Kohlberg's thinking and research on moral development. If we look beyond the oft-found accusations that Kohlberg (and Piaget before him, or others working within a developmental tradition) had no interest in behavior or that he sacrificed the action component, deemed to be the most central to morality, for the exclusive study of judgment, it becomes abundantly evident that from the beginning of his career he was seriously grappling with the problem of the coordination of judgment and action in the developmental process. It is also ironic that Kohlberg was, directly or indirectly, engaged in empirical study of judgment-action relationships as much as, if not more than, anyone else in the past three decades. These efforts, however, cannot be characterized as a search for the straightforward, conventional connection between judgment and action. Instead, as the title of this chapter suggests, he was pursuing the bi-directional coordination of thought and action in the developmental process.

It is more than a historical or sociological curiosity that the impression is often conveyed that Kohlberg was unconcerned with action while his published (and some unpublished) works reflect a life-long concern with action. The contradiction is of special interest because it illuminates important aspects of different perspectives on the role of action in moral development. That it is thought Kohlberg was unconcerned with behavior is illustrated by the assertion that in Kohlberg's theory a "dependence on deductive logic may be responsible for its proponents' lack of interest in action research" (Haan, 1978, p. 290). Moreover, this presumed lack of interest is judged to be particularly serious because "moral action, not thought, is society's ultimate criterion of moral wisdom as well as social science's test of a conceptualization's validity" (Haan, 1978, p. 296). In a similar vein, it has recently been asserted that "most of the recent psychological interest in the domain of morality has centered on analyses of moral thought. The conspicuous neglect of moral conduct reflects both the rationalistic bias of many theories of morality and the convenience of investigatory methods. It is considerably easier to examine how people reason about hypothetical moral dilemmas than to study their actual moral conduct. People suffer from the wrongs done to them however perpetrators might justify their inhumane action" (Bandura, in press, p. 1).

It is accurate to say that Kohlberg did not regard action, in opposition to thought, as the ultimate criterion of morality or as the ultimate test of validity. He viewed matters as more complicated than that. However, his theory did not have a dependence on deductive logic (though he took it into account) and he certainly regarded action as important. Contrary to the misconception that "surprisingly little attention [has been given] to the relationship between moral reasoning and moral conduct" (Bandura, in press, p. 28) within the tradition Kohlberg did much to foster, there have been many studies on action and its relation to judgment.

These false impressions may stem from Kohlberg's continuous emphasis on thoroughly explicating, through several revisions, the course of the development of moral judgments, as well as his conviction that behavior could not be understood without a concomitant understanding of judgments and development. Kohlberg's early critiques of behaviorism may have also contributed to a misconstrual of his orientation to action. On a personal note, I rapidly learned in 1960, when I began graduate study at Yale in developmental and social psychology, that Kohlberg's criticisms of behaviorism and radical empiricism were combined with an abiding concern with judgment, action, and development. The early 1960s was a time of transition from the dominance of behaviorism— methodological and theoretical—to the emergence of approaches that seriously analyzed individuals' judgments in ways going beyond assessment of surface attitudes. The field of developmental psychology was becoming immersed in those changes, largely stimulated by the research and theories of Piaget (who had actually put forth nonbehaviorist positions many years earlier). As a young assistant professor at Yale, Kohlberg was quickly becoming a major figure at the forefront of a cognitive, developmental, and philosophically oriented movement. His contributions were methodological (opening up methods for the study of reasoning that are now standard practice), theoretical (especially regarding structure and development), and substantive (with regard to social development). In addition to morality, Kohlberg was proposing new approaches to sex-role development, influences of child-rearing practices, and processes of identification and imitation.

Moral Action from a Nonbehavioristic Perspective

In the early 1960s, the dominant themes regarding moral acquisition were still that behavior was the proper central focus of investigation, but assessments could be made of attitudes, preference, and knowledge of cultural norms or values as a means of measuring the consistency or inconsistency between behavior and verbally expressed values. It was also commonly assumed in those behavioristically oriented perspectives that such measures of verbal values were not predictive of behavior. As summarized by Aronfreed (1968, p. 9), measures of attitudes and preferences were not highly correlated with behavioral measures: "Although it is generally assumed that values are the most significant source of control over social conduct . . . , the available evidence usually points to great discrepancies between children's verbal expression of evaluative standards and their actual behavior in a real social context. . . . Knowledge of the standards of conduct to which a child subscribes will often not permit an accurate prediction of its behavior under conditions where the child is not exposed to the surveillance or reactions of external agents of control."

In general agreement with the dominant orientation of the time (and with newly emerging social learning perspectives), Kohlberg believed that the construct of general internal dispositions, in the form of moral character traits, was inadequate for explaining relations between behavior and verbally espoused moral values. In one extant nonbehavioristic perspective of those times, morality was approached from the viewpoint of the acquisition of a set of traits of character (Havighurst and Taba, 1949; Jones, 1936; Peck and Havighurst, 1960). At an earlier time, Hartshorne and May's (1928-1930) classic research had shown that the usual list of character traits (for example, honesty, service, self-control) neither resulted in the expected consistencies in behaviors across situations nor produced clear correlations between such internal dispositions and behavior.

Whereas Kohlberg accepted the negative findings regarding the influences of internal dispositions on behavior, he was by no means convinced that such evidence bore on the more general question of individuals' "internal" moral constructs. He also was not content to leave assessments of internal constructs at the level of surface content. At the time, one purported virtue of measures of attitudes, preferences, and knowledge of cultural values was that they are relatively easy to operationalize, translate into paper and pencil assessments, and thereby correlate with equally easy to operationalize measures of behavior. Kohlberg (1963, 1964) forcefully argued that this is an empty virtue if, as was becoming increasingly recognized in the late 1950s and early 1960s, such measures failed to capture the essence of human thought, which goes beyond surface content or static traits.

The movement toward the study of processes of thought underlying content took several forms. One of those was a focus on the structures or organizations of thought hypothesized to emerge out of an individual's reciprocal interactions with social and physical environments, including the person's reflections as a concomitant of direct, immediate experiences. This structural and interactional perspective requires that assessments of judgments go beyond surface content. It also entails identification and study of nontrivial actions that are part of the domain under investigation, specification of criteria for assessing appropriate correspondences between types of judgments and types of actions, and examination of how situations are construed from the perspective of individuals' structures of thought.

All four of these considerations have been part of the structural-developmental agenda. Kohlberg's initial investigations of moral judgments, through the use of hypothetical dilemmas, included the study of how individuals construe situational contexts. Along with Piaget (1932) and gestalt-oriented social psychologists (for example, Asch, 1952; Duncker, 1939; Lewin, 1935), Kohlberg was exploring how individuals construe different types of social situational contexts. This was one motivation for his well-known innovation of posing to subjects hypothetical conflicts between different social or moral considerations, such as between legality and values of life, equality, or property, or between authority and individual rights. Whereas individuals would generally value property and condemn stealing, and value life and endorse its preservation, as examples, their judgments about these types of issues might vary in accordance with how they construe particular situational contexts (such as a context in which saving a life might require violating property rights). In contrast with content assessments of preferences, or with knowledge-tapping endorsement or condemnation of moral prescriptions and proscriptions, the use of conflicts provided sufficiently rich situational contexts for the study of variations in moral precepts. These procedures constitute stimulus contexts for examining how individuals perceive social situations and apply their moral concepts, which in turn allow for the type of probes that elicit responses reflecting the organization of judgments.

The structural perspective on an individual's construal of social situations classifies morality as a fundamental epistemological realm in which action cannot be disassociated from judgment. Although philosophers had traditionally treated morality as an epistemological realm, from the psychological perspective it had generally been treated as the means by which individual behavior is controlled and shaped. Accordingly, the study of the control of behavior did not bring with it examination of the nature of the realm under investigation (see Chomsky, 1975, and Piaget, 1970 for further discussion of the need for coordination of psychological and epistemological analyses). Defining the nature of the moral realm is relevant to the study of action as well as judgment. In pursuing the hypothesis that action and judgment are interrelated, it is essential that situational contexts for the study of action be at levels of complexity comparable to the complexity of judgments brought to bear on those situations.

These considerations were primary in Kohlberg's approach to moral development. A central premise, simply put, was the nonbehavioristic proposition that to understand action it is also necessary to understand judgment: "We can only discuss morality of action when we relate the actor's behavior to his actual judgments of right and wrong in the situation. So far no research has ever undertaken such an analysis. The reason it has not been done has been because of skepticism as to the correspondence of conduct and moral verbalization. This skepticism is justified as long as the relationship of moral judgment to action is interpreted in terms of defining both verbalization and action as a matter of strength or intensity of a moral attitude against cheating" (Kohlberg, 1965, p. 3).

In his initial formulations, Kohlberg introduced an important shift in thinking about judgment and action. His analyses demonstrated that the variations typically found in cheating behaviors (a frequently studied behavior at the time) could be explained in terms of associations with meanings attributed to particular situations, including the child's interpretation of an experimenter's expectations. Perhaps best bringing the issue home to researchers was the observation that psychologists "have cheated children time and again by lying to them and saying they were unobserved while observing their cheating behavior. Yet, all of us, I hope, could argue that our cheating was consistent with our moral principles, and we refrain from cheating under ordinary conditions" (Kohlberg, 1965, p. 3). The point, of course, was that intensity or strength of attitudes toward values of honesty, per se, fails to account for different types of meanings given to situations. A series of studies on cheating behaviors by Kohlberg and his colleagues demonstrated that while verbalized strength of attitudes or beliefs did not correlate with behavior, measures of moral reasoning relevant to cheating situations, such as trust, contract, social agreement, and merit or effort, showed closer relations to cheating behavior in children and adolescents.

This focus on assessment of cheating behaviors was mainly in reaction to the behavioristically oriented research being conducted at the time. Subsequently, Kohlberg expanded his concerns to the need to connect psychological and developmental analyses of action, as well as judgment, to philosophically oriented epistemological analyses and to the need to assess meaningful moral behaviors: "There is no valid psychological definition of moral behavior in the sense that no observation and categorization of a behavior from the outside or 'behavioristically' can define its moral status in any psychologically valid sense" (Kohlberg, 1969, p. 8).

The assertion that there is no valid psychological definition of moral behavior from the "outside" can be taken either as consistent with relativistic viewpoints or as a radical departure from past practice in research on moral action. It could be consistent with relativistic views of morality in the sense that morality is said to be strictly a subjective phenomenon: moral behavior is what the actor considers to be moral behavior, which can vary from person to person. Given Kohlberg's persistent and pointed advocacy of nonrelativistic positions (see especially Kohlberg, 1971), some other interpretation of this assertion must hold. The assertion was, indeed, a radical departure from past practice. In most cases, the behaviors investigated were chosen without explicit criteria regarding their moral status and without assessments of how the subject construed the moral status of the act or reasoned about it. Kohlberg's approach, as reflected in the above-quoted assertion, was that in order to study moral behavior it is necessary to determine subjects' judgments and to provide criteria for classifying the actions within the moral domain.

Features of Situational Contexts

A close look at Kohlberg's early formulations concretely illustrates the fundamental concepts regarding the role of epistemological criteria, the relation of the individual's judgments in the context of situations, and the inadequacy of defining moral behavior from the outside. With regard to what may have appeared as simple and straightforward studies of honesty through cheating behavior, Kohlberg pointed out some of the complexities of these factors. In particular, the lack of systematic definitions of honesty, coupled with varying implicit definitions, resulted in a failure to specify the parameters of the tasks used to assess behavior (what has come to be referred to as "task analyses"). For instance, the research of Hartshorne and May (1928-1930) included presenting children with testlike and gamelike competitive situations in which they had the opportunity to deceive the experimenter by altering their performance (experimenters acted so as to convey the impression to the children that their cheating would be undetected). By operationalizing honesty through such cheating behaviors several important situational features are ignored. First is the problem of whether the situation is meaningful to the children. Kohlberg contended that most experimental cheating situations are perceived by children either as trivial (they are "Mickey Mouse" was his colloquial way of putting it) or unfathomable. This is because the experimental situations are seen as contrived, with no apparent purpose, in unfamiliar contexts and expectations. Further, the experimenter's behavior implicitly conveys the impression that the situation is not taken seriously (for example, leaving children unsupervised when they normally are not) and that there is no authority exerted: "There is . . . a . . . basic ambiguity in the situation. The ambiguity is the ambiguity as to whether anyone cares or not. Not only does the experimenter indicate he doesn't care whether cheating goes on, he almost suggests its possibility and desirability" (Kohlberg, 1969, p. 19). By concentrating on the problem of creating situations that provide children with the impression that their transgressions will go undetected, researchers ignored the child's perspective on the situations and the moral status of the contexts created.

The results of most of these types of studies strongly suggest that children do process the message that the experimenter "does not care" and that behavior is primarily guided by nonmoral considerations. As is well known, studies of honesty, including those of Hartshorne and May, have typically shown that children cheat much of the time. Subsequent and more technically sophisticated experiments have yielded the same result. For example, Grinder (1961, 1962), who had seventh-graders compete using a ray gun to obtain a marksmanship prize, found that 80 percent of them deceptively changed their scores. A follow-up study by Lehrer (1967), done in collaboration with Kohlberg, demonstrated that extrinsic factors (detection, praise, and blame) are highly determinative of children's behaviors in cheating situations. Lehrer's use of machinery giving the impression that it would be difficult to engage in undetected cheating resulted in only 15 percent of the children cheating.

This is not to say that there are no moral components in experimental situations aimed at measuring honesty. Components of agreement, trust, contract, and equal opportunity can all apply to these situations. The experiments, however, were constructed so that certain situational features (the perceived unimportance of the act and experimenters' acquiescence) overrode moral considerations for many children. Additional studies by Kohlberg and his colleagues (Grim, Kohlberg, and White, 1968; Krebs, 1967) showed that types of moral judgment, as measured by stage, correlated with behavior. Subjects at the higher stages of moral judgment cheated considerably less than those at lower stages. However, there was not a one-to-one correspondence between stage and behavior. Kohlberg proposed that in interaction with judgments and situational features, actions are mediated by ego factors such as attention and willpower.

It should be stressed that in this perspective several aspects of judgment are at work. Clearly, one is the subject's structure of moral judgments. Another is the subject's interpretation of the situation at hand, and the process of coordinating judgments about the situation with perhaps more general moral concepts held. The perspective was summarized by Kohlberg (1969, p. 7) as follows:

> To label children's performance on Hartshorne and May's cheating tests as dishonest is as ambiguous and relative as it is to label Hartshorne and May dishonest for giving such tests. Furthermore, there are no definitions a psychologist can give qua psychologist in the clash of value-perspectives. A lawyer called me up to ask whether I could provide a psychological definition of conscience which would certify an act of draft-resistance as an act of conscience. The answer is, of course, "no," there is no purely psychological definition of conscience which could indicate that a morally principled act of draft resistance is psychologically different than Sirhan's murder of Kennedy on the behest of his "superego." To use a simpler case, Edmund Wilson (and Thoreau) failed to pay income taxes as a "matter of conscience," while millions of their fellow citizens fail to do so for reasons of "expedience." The behaviors are the same and no psychologist can tell the behavior apart; it is only what the people involved think they are doing which sets the behavior apart.

Leaving it solely at the level of the subject's interpretation of the moral status of the act, however, would lead to relativism and an unacceptable tautology. The relativism is that if only the actor's judgment about the moral status of the act were considered, then any action consistent with the actor's classification and judgment would have to be said to be a moral action. The tautological aspect is that a moral action is any action judged to be a moral action. This type of tautology is reminiscent of operational definitions of the sort provided in the psychometric tradition of intelligence testing, that is, intelligence is what an intelligence test measures. As Piaget (1947) has demonstrated, such operational definitions of intelligence are unsatisfactory both because the nature of the construct is left unspecified and because they fail to provide a basis for assessing the types, rather than amount, of intelligence developed by individuals.

Similarly, to avoid the tautology, as well as the relativism, other factors must be included in the study of morality. In particular, it is necessary to assess the actions and situations in ways that are not solely the actor's assessments (though those must be included). One risk in this enterprise, however, is that the "independent" assessments of actions and situations merely reduces to an imposition of the researcher's own moral judgments. This, in turn, can be avoided by providing a theoretical framework that includes general criteria for the moral realm and for actions. That is, epistemological analyses of morality represent a means for specifying criteria of judgment and actions as a basis for analyzing subjects' judgments and actions. It was because of these considerations that Kohlberg concerned himself more extensively than most psychologists with issues of "is to ought," with philosophical analyses of the psychology of moral development.

In some respects, Kohlberg's venture into philosophical analyses was a reluctant one because of his recognition that interdisciplinary efforts required the collaboration of scholars from the different disciplines. As he half-facetiously put it, "Now, obviously a developmental psychologist must be a fool to enter the den of philosophical wolves with a set of 'Is to Ought' claims unless he has to" (Kohlberg, 1971, p. 153). This reluctance is apparent in Kohlberg's restriction of the task of philosophical analysis to one of providing basic criteria of the moral realm to inform studies of psychological functions and acquisition. Kohlberg used such criteria, in combination with his formulations of the most advanced stages of moral development, in the context of his analyses of the interaction of the individual and the situation.

Kohlberg's early analyses of the existing research on moral action indeed resulted in a reconceptualization of the judgment-action problem, at least from a structural and interactional perspective. The formulations established a research agenda that includes serious consideration of the nature and processes of moral and other social judgments, even if one's primary concern is with explication of action. For this reason, many have concentrated on research into the development of judgments (in their shifting process of coordinating study of judgment and of action). Some of these studies are in the context of Kohlberg's propositions and assessments of moral judgment stages. However, for many researchers working within a structural tradition this has entailed analyses of action in relation to judgment, as well as the coordination of the two. Kohlberg's reconceptualization of action and his formulation of a fruitful research agenda is clearly seen in many studies of moral behavior, including those conducted by researchers who do not necessarily agree with either his specific or general characterizations of moral judgments (Blasi, 1983; Damon, 1977; Gilligan, 1982; Haan, 1978, 1986; Krebs and Rosenwald, 1977; Selman, 1980, 1981; Smetana, 1982; Turiel, 1983; Turiel and Smetana, 1984).

The balance of Kohlberg's empirical and analytic efforts were on the judgment side of the pendulum. In that context, however, Kohlberg had a substantial involvement in research on action. One general facet of these research efforts had the aim of identifying actions that would be meaningful from the subject's point of view and from the perspective of valid definitions of the moral realm. The search for assessments of meaningful actions is important both from the viewpoint of how judgment might influence actions and from the viewpoint of how actions might influence development (Piaget, 1932). Toward these aims, Kohlberg and his colleagues grappled with a series of naturalistic and experimental situations that intuitively, and by virtue of analyses of the parameters of the tasks, met the criteria of meaningfulness for the subject and consistency with the epistemological status of the domain.

The first study of this sort was conducted by Kohlberg with the cooperation of Stanley Milgram, his colleague at Yale in the early 1960s. Milgram had just begun to obtain the now well-known findings that adults can be led to inflict intense physical harm on another person at the instructions of an insistent experimenter. This experimental situation was clearly nontrivial, as Kohlberg was quick to recognize. It entailed physical harm, as well as a conflict between a moral concern for avoiding harm to another and strong external pressures to obey the implicit rules of the situation and the explicit commands of an authority. Moreover, the experiment highlights the interaction between the person and features of social situations. Data were obtained showing a general correspondence between moral judgment stage and behavior (higher-stage subjects were more likely to defy the experimenter than were lower-stage subjects). Again, there was not a complete correspondence between stage and behavior.

Similar findings were obtained in several other studies of natural actions in situations with real consequences. A number of studies looked at the moral judgments of juvenile delinquents (Kohlberg, 1958; Kohlberg and Freundlich, 1972; see Blasi, 1980, for a review). Studies were also done with college students engaging in civil disobedience over issues of rights and justice (Haan, Smith, and Block, 1968). Analyses were conducted of public discussions by participants in the Watergate affair, which resulted in Richard Nixon's resignation as president of the United States (Candee, 1976). Public pronouncements from, as well as interviews with, participants in the killing of children and adult civilians at My Lai during the Vietnam War were also analyzed (Kohlberg and Candee, 1984). In addition, judgments have been related to behavior in the contexts of prison life (Kohlberg, Scharf, and Hickey, 1972) and participation in morally relevant school activities (Kohlberg, 1980, 1985; Kohlberg and Higgins, 1987; Power, 1988). Much of this research is correlational in nature, but it provides empirical documentation that judgment and action are related. Indeed, a comprehensive review of the research by Blasi (1980, p. 10) leads to a conclusion opposite to the conventional wisdom: "Those who find these considerations sensible and convincing and who are aware of the limitations of the available studies in representing the moral complexities will be surprised by the extent to which the empirical literature supports the hypothesis of a significant relationship between moral thinking and moral behavior. To a large extent, the opposite opinion, that moral reasoning and moral behavior are independent dimensions, is revealed to be a well-advertised myth."

The documentation of a relationship between moral judgment and action stems mainly from correlational studies. Several features of the correlational research are important to note. One is that although judgment and action are related, the body of evidence shows that the correlational levels vary. A range of correlational levels have been obtained, but it is rare that they demonstrate a strict correspondence of moral judgment to action. Thus, it is not very often that action can be predicted directly from knowledge of individuals' moral judgments. There is also contextual variability in the judgment-action relationship since the correlational levels differ in accordance with the situation. Thus, there is evidence for both consistencies and inconsistencies between moral judgment and action. Moreover, correlational studies only serve to provide empirical assessments of the extent of consistency or inconsistency; data on consistency levels do not yield an explanation of the nature of the relationship between judgment and action. Recognizing the explanatory limitations of correlational studies and seeking to account for other variables that contribute to the relationship, Kohlberg and others (for example, Blasi, 1983; Haan, 1986) attempted to identify psychological factors that mediate between judgment and action. In what has turned out to be an inconclusive fashion, Kohlberg has tested several hypotheses. The studies on honesty lead him to postulate that personality features, such as ego strength, attention, and willpower, mediate between judgment and action. He also proposed that these mediating variables are more of a factor for subjects at lower than at higher stages of moral development (Kohlberg, 1971). In subsequent research (Kohlberg and Candee, 1984), he proposed that moral judgments of autonomy and responsibility, as different moral processes from the concepts associated with the stages, mediated between judgment and action.

In these explanations of action the emphasis has been on moral judgments and not on other kinds of social judgments. Insofar as moral judgments are not entirely consistent with action, the search is for noncognitive psychological variables that might contribute to action. However, an alternative proposition, consistent with the structural and developmental concepts put forth by Kohlberg, would pay greater attention to the role of nonmoral social judgments in social actions. If an individual's construal of situational contexts is relevant to action, then analyses of thought should not necessarily be restricted to moral judgments. The scope of the types of judgments brought to bear on situations entailing action needs to be broadened to include other, nonmoral social judgments. Correspondingly, the epistemological task is made more complicated by the necessity of identifying and defining both moral and nonmoral aspects of social situations.

Coordination of Social and Moral Judgments in Social Contexts

In spite of the empirical evidence, skepticism still exists about the role of moral judgments in behavior. There are several reasons, no doubt, for skepticism about judgment-action relations. Perhaps some observers are unaware of the overall body of evidence, focusing solely on those studies yielding low or moderate correlations. Some may even base their evaluations on criticism of the design of the typical studies. However, there is a deeper skepticism about the moral judgment dimension itself. For some, judgments are merely epiphenomena that are at best irrelevant to moral action and at worst often manipulated by actors to rationalize and place in a positive light their highly immoral actions. Scrutiny of this type of skepticism is informative because it actually serves to illustrate the importance of some of the themes considered thus far: the need for careful analyses of individuals' judgmental perspectives on situations, as well as for conceptually powerful analyses and definitions of the moral domain. It further serves to highlight the need for analyses that look at the coordination of different types of social judgments in behavioral outcomes.

Examples of deep skepticism about human moral reasoning can be seen in social learning perspectives. A particularly succinct statement of it was provided by Mischel and Mischel (1976, p. 107) in their early exposition of a cognitive social-learning approach to morality.

> The same individual who espouses high moral principles may engage in harmful aggressive actions against others who violate his conceptions of justice. . . . History is replete with atrocities that were justified by invoking the highest principles and that were perpetrated upon victims who were equally convinced of their own moral principles. In the name of justice, of the common welfare, of universal ethics, and of God, millions of people have been killed and whole cultures destroyed. In recent history, concepts of universal right, equality, freedom, and social equity have been used to justify every variety of murder including genocide.

The idea is that if moral justifications can be invoked to support evil or immoral behaviors, then they cannot be of utility in explaining moral action. This line of thought was more recently carried forth within cognitive social-learning theory by Bandura (in press). His premises are that "people do not ordinarily engage in reprehensible conduct until they have justified to themselves the morality of their actions" and that "what is culpable can be made righteous through cognitive reconstrual" (p. 35). A litany of examples are given of morally reprehensible and culpable actions that are typically justified with positively couched moral principles (pp. 35-44). For instance, exploitation, killing, and restriction of freedoms are said to often occur in the name of moral principles, as well as religious and nationalistic imperatives: "Over the years, much reprehensible and destructive conduct has been perpetuated by ordinary, decent people in the name of religious principles, righteous ideologies, and nationalistic imperatives" (p. 36). Additional evidence of the idea that moral justifications serve to explain away favored actions comes from a series of examples of currently debated issues in which disputants provide moral principles to support diametrically opposed positions. Principles are invoked to support social reform by those out of power or the status quo by those in power; civil disobedience or social control; and terrorism or counterterrorism. Similarly, both sides of the argument regarding the development and stockpiling of nuclear weapons invoke moral arguments and justifications to support their propositions.

These assertions and examples slight over several issues important to serious analyses of morality. For instance, moral disputes, including the assertion of principles on two sides of an issue, may reflect more on the legitimate conflicts endemic to social and moral interactions than on the rationalization of justifications. As another example, the notion that immoral acts are committed in the name of religion or nationalism is in contradiction with the relativistic view, generally embraced by social learning theorists, that morality entails adherence to learned religious, societal, or cultural norms.

Also, it is not explicitly stated whether the supposed rationalizations of supposed immoral actions are hypocritical or genuinely believed by their proponents. If hypocrisy was solely at issue, the task would be to provide means for discriminating between falsely espoused and real beliefs. To do so, even in that case, we would need accurate formulations of persons' moral judgments. Apparently, however, the skepticism about these judgments runs deeper in that it is thought that evil actions are justified with genuinely held moral principles. The claims of this type of skepticism could only be supported with empirical studies that include epistemological analyses of the domain, task analyses of behavioral situations, and explanations of individuals' judgments.

By invoking moral claims the argument requires analyses of the moral domain. It is maintained that certain actions are reprehensible, culpable, evil, and immoral. Other actions are described as destructive, inhumane, violent, and atrocious. Since the moral status of these actions is evaluated independently of the actors' judgments, their morality is being characterized from the "outside" or behavioristically. The argument amounts to a nonrelativistic, moralistic assertion of the rightness and wrongness of actions that can be characterized independently of the actors' perspectives (as well as cultural perspectives, insofar as religious and nationalistic imperatives are deemed to sometimes be rationalizations for evil acts).

It is solely the researchers' own value judgments, however, that serve to classify the behaviors since no explicit definitions or criteria of moral status are provided. Although we may intuit, along with the researchers, that many of the actions cited are wrong (evil, atrocious, and so on), as part of social scientific analyses of behavior and development our moral intuitions are insufficient. Again, it is necessary to provide an epistemological analysis that includes systematic criteria for the classification of actions. Otherwise, we are simply left with an imposition of the researchers' own value judgments.

Empirical study of moral action would place the definitional criteria into a context of analyses of the parameters of concrete situations in which specific behaviors are assessed. For the most part, however, the skeptical arguments have been based on anecdotal evidence, albeit several of the examples come from public and historical sources. Furthermore, the bases for the assertion that certain moral justifications or principles have been used to support the immoral actions are unclear since no documentation is provided. Insofar as there is any reference to empirical findings (Bandura, in press), it comes from experiments like those of Milgram. The example of subjects inflicting physical harm on others is invoked to show that even "decent" people can engage in destructive behaviors.

However, a close look at the findings from Milgram's experiments, along with criteria for social domains and task analyses, reveals a different picture from the skeptical view. It illustrates the relevance of social and moral conflicts, as well as a significant role for individuals' judgments (Turiel, 1983; Turiel and Smetana, 1984). The Milgram experiments are especially useful for these purposes because they allow us to focus on more than final behavioral actions. The actions and interactions occurred over time within the experimental situations. The conflicts experienced, the social pressures placed on subjects, and the subjects' deliberations were all observable as the experiments proceeded.

First, it has been documented (Milgram, 1974) that subjects struggled with their behavioral decisions. They did not blithely engage in action, merely rationalizing it with moral justifications. Rather, most subjects, including and especially those who thought they were inflicting harm by continuing to administer electric shocks to the victim, acted with much conflict, reluctance, and vacillation. To understand the subjects' conflict and the reasons for their actions, it is necessary to examine the components of the social situations confronted. The experimental situations constructed by Milgram were multifaceted, including at least two basic types of social considerations. One pertains to inflicting harm, since subjects were instructed to administer powerful shocks to another human being. The second component pertains to the social organization of the situation. There were strong external pressures to adhere to the explicit commands of an authority and to the implicit rules of a situation with scientific aims.

The behaviors of the subjects reflect a conflict between these two components. The conflict and vacillation manifested by subjects who continued to administer shocks was over adherence to the rules and authority dictates, on the one hand, and concern with the other person's welfare, on the other hand. Correspondingly, those who refused to continue administering the shocks were conflicted because of their reluctance to disrupt the experiment or thwart its scientific goals. Viewed in this context, subjects' actions are not appropriately regarded as "reprehensible" or "culpable" conduct made righteous or acceptable through cognitive reconstrual. More to the point is that subjects were construing and coordinating what they considered different legitimate social considerations in an inherent conflict. Each actor's moral and nonmoral judgments about the situation are essential components.

There is a good deal of evidence that children form distinct domains of social judgment corresponding to the components identified in the Milgram experimental situations (Turiel, 1983; Turiel, Killen, and Helwig, 1987). Moral judgments pertaining to harm, justice, and rights constitute a domain distinct from understandings of social rules, authority, and conventions in social organization. In contrast with the skeptical view of judgment, accounting for these domains and their coordination would allow for more precise understandings of consistencies and inconsistencies between judgment and action. Most likely, we would need to have elaborate conceptualizations of simultaneous consistencies and inconsistencies. For instance, it can be said that in the Milgram experiments those who continued to shock the other person acted in ways inconsistent with their moral judgments about harm. At the same time, their actions could be said to be consistent with their judgments regarding social organization. The reverse holds for those who refused to shock. Whereas the behavior was consistent with their moral judgments, it may have been inconsistent with their judgments regarding social organization.

These potential patterns of consistency and inconsistency are rendered even more complex by the findings of situational variations in behavior across experimental conditions (Milgram, 1974). In contrast with the well-known finding from one condition (Milgram, 1963) that a majority continued to shock the victim, in several other conditions most subjects (100 percent, in some cases) actively refused to obey the experimenter and ceased to inflict harm on another. This situational variability was not simply due to different contexts mechanically eliciting different behaviors. Behavioral shifts were associated with systematic variations in the salience of either the harm component or the social organizational component. In brief (see Turiel and Smetana, 1984, for details), increases in salience of moral features (for example, greater visibility of the victim) or decreases in the salience of social organization features (for example, diffusion of the authority's jurisdiction) resulted in a majority of subjects defying the experimenter's instructions.

The findings of variations in behaviors associated with systematic shifts in parameters of the situation provide evidence for the proposition that actions are based on judgments brought to bear on social contexts. How individuals construe social situations depends on an interaction of situational features and different types or domains of reasoning held by them. To determine how situations are construed, both the individuals' judgments and situational features must be specified. Moreover, we cannot rely solely on analyses of moral judgments. Different types of social judgments can be applicable to most social situations.

Conclusion

The proposition that judgment-action relations involve a coordination of distinctly different domains of social judgment differs in certain ways from the approach pursued by Lawrence Kohlberg in his pathbreaking work on moral development. In my view, Kohlberg's almost exclusive emphasis on the moral aspects of social interactions led him away from other significant social domains and from consideration of nonmoral, but yet social, judgments essential to an exploration of how moral judgments are related to action. Nevertheless, Kohlberg's formulations must be viewed as setting the stage for these types of analyses of action, as well as other nonbehavioristic approaches. Indeed, Kohlberg's incisive propositions have served to highlight central considerations regarding the study of moral action in ways that guide current and, no doubt, future research.

However, behavioristic biases still exist, as reflected in the skeptical view of judgment just mentioned. Proponents of that skeptical view could fill some fundamental gaps by paying greater attention to the need for epistemological definition of domains, task analyses of behavioral contexts, and examination of individuals' perspectives on their actions. As stated at the outset, in addition, the myth persists that Kohlberg and other proponents of a structural and developmental approach are uninterested in moral action. It seems that concentration on analyses of judgment is falsely taken by some to represent a lack of concern with behavior. This is a misrepresentation of Kohlberg's position since clearly he provided insightful formulations and empirical directions for the study of action. It would benefit the field of developmental psychology if Kohlberg's messages regarding judgment and action were adequately assimilated. One important manifestation of this inadequate assimilation is the recent call in our field for a movement away from the study of reflective judgments through hypothetical situations as stimuli, in favor of study of only behavior and judgments in context, or so-called real-life situations. Whereas the study of judgments in context is important (Damon, 1977; Kohlberg and Higgins, 1987; Selman, 1980; Turiel, Smetana, and Killen, in press), it should not be turned into a special virtue to be done at the exclusion of the equally important study of reflective judgments. Kohlberg demonstrated that research on reflective judgments can be a powerful way of providing the theoretical basis needed for study of action in context.

References

Aronfreed, J. *Conduct and Conscience: The Socialization of Internalized Control over Behavior.* New York: Academic Press, 1968.
Asch, S. *Social Psychology.* Englewood Cliffs, N.J.: Prentice-Hall, 1952.
Bandura, A. "Social Cognitive Theory of Moral Thought and Action." In W. M. Kurtines and J. L. Gewirtz (eds.), *Handbook of Moral Behavior and Development.* Vol. 1: *Theory.* Hillsdale, N.J.: Erlbaum, in press.
Blasi, A. "Bridging Moral Cognition and Action: A Critical Review of the Literature." *Psychological Bulletin,* 1980, *88,* 1–45.
Blasi, A. "Moral Cognition and Moral Action: A Theoretical Perspective." *Developmental Review,* 1983, *3,* 178–210.
Candee, D. "Structure and Choice in Moral Reasoning." *Journal of Personality and Social Psychology,* 1976, *34,* 1293–1301.
Chomsky, N. *Reflections on Language.* New York: Pantheon, 1975.
Damon, W. *The Social World of the Child.* San Francisco: Jossey-Bass, 1977.
Duncker, K. "Ethical Relativity? (An Enquiry into the Psychology of Ethics)." *Mind,* 1939, *48,* 39–53.
Gilligan, C. *In a Different Voice: Psychological Theory and Women's Development.* Cambridge, Mass.: Harvard University Press, 1982.
Grim, P. F., Kohlberg, L., and White, S. H. "Some Relationships Between Conscience and Attentional Processes." *Journal of Personality and Social Psychology,* 1968, *8,* 239–252.
Grinder, R. E. "New Techniques for Research in Children's Concepts of Justice." *Child Development,* 1961, *32,* 679–683.
Grinder, R. E. "Parental Child-Rearing Practices, Conscience and Resistance to Temptation of Sixth Grade Children." *Child Development,* 1962, *33,* 802–820.
Haan, N. "Two Moralities in Action Contexts: Relationship to Thought, Ego Regulation, and Development." *Journal of Personality and Social Psychology,* 1978, *36,* 286–305.
Haan, N. "Systematic Variability in the Quality of Moral Action, as Defined in Two Formulations." *Journal of Personality and Social Psychology,* 1986, *50,* 1271–1284.
Haan, N., Smith, M. B., and Block, J. "Moral Reasoning of Young Adults: Political-Social Behavior, Family Background, and Personality Correlates." *Journal of Personality and Social Psychology,* 1968, *10,* 183–201.

Hartshorne, H., and May, M. S. *Studies in the Nature of Character.* Vol. 1: *Studies in Deceit;* Vol. 2: *Studies in Self-Control;* Vol. 3: *Studies in the Organization of Character.* New York: Macmillan, 1928, 1929, 1930.

Havighurst, R., and Taba, H. *Adolescent Character and Personality.* New York: Wiley, 1949.

Jones, V. *Character and Citizenship Training in the Public Schools.* Chicago: University of Chicago Press, 1936.

Kohlberg, L. "The Development of Modes of Moral Thinking and Choice in the Years 10 to 16." Unpublished doctoral dissertation, University of Chicago, 1958.

Kohlberg, L. "Moral Development and Identification." In H. Stevenson (ed.), *Child Psychology: 62nd Yearbook of the National Society for the Study of Education.* Chicago: University of Chicago Press, 1963.

Kohlberg, L. "Development of Moral Character and Moral Ideology." In M. L. Hoffman and L. W. Hoffman (eds.), *Review of Child Development Research.* Vol. 1. New York: Russell Sage Foundation, 1964.

Kohlberg, L. "Relationships Between the Development of Moral Judgments and Moral Conduct." Paper presented at the biannual meeting of the Society for Research in Child Development. Minneapolis, Minnesota, March 1965.

Kohlberg, L. "The Relations Between Moral Judgment and Action: A Developmental View." Paper presented at the Institute of Human Development, University of California, Berkeley, March 1969.

Kohlberg, L. "From Is to Ought: How to Commit the Naturalistic Fallacy and Get Away with It in the Study of Moral Development." In T. Mischel (ed.), *Cognitive Development and Epistemology.* New York: Academic Press, 1971.

Kohlberg, L. "High School Democracy and Educating for a Just Society." In R. Mosher (ed.), *Moral Education: A First Generation of Research and Development.* New York: Praeger, 1980.

Kohlberg, L., and Candee, D. "The Relationship of Moral Judgment to Moral Action." In L. Kohlberg, *Essays on Moral Development.* Vol. 2: *The Psychology of Moral Development.* New York: Harper & Row, 1984.

Kohlberg, L., and Freundlich, D. "Moral Judgment in Youthful Offenders." Unpublished manuscript, Graduate School of Education, Harvard University, 1972.

Kohlberg, L., and Higgins, A. "School Democracy and Social Interaction." In W. M. Kurtines and J. L. Gewirtz (eds.), *Moral Development Through Social Interaction.* New York: Wiley, 1987.

Kohlberg, L., Scharf, P., and Hickey, J. "The Justice Structure of the Prison: A Theory and Intervention." *Prison Journal,* 1972, *51,* 3-14.

Krebs, D., and Rosenwald, A. "Moral Reasoning and Moral Behavior in Conventional Adults." *Merrill-Palmer Quarterly,* 1977, *23,* 79-84.

Krebs, R. "Some Relationships Between Moral Judgment, Attention, and Resistance to Temptation." Unpublished doctoral dissertation, University of Chicago, 1967.

Lehrer, L. "Sex Differences in Moral Behavior and Attitudes." Unpublished doctoral dissertation, University of Chicago, 1967.

Lewin, K. *A Dynamic Theory of Personality.* New York: McGraw-Hill, 1985.

Milgram, S. "Behavioral Study of Obedience." *Journal of Abnormal and Social Psychology,* 1963, *67,* 371-378.

Milgram, S. *Obedience to Authority.* New York: Harper & Row, 1974.

Mischel, W., and Mischel, H. N. "A Cognitive Social-Learning Approach to Morality and Self-Regulation." In T. Lickona (ed.), *Moral Development: Theory, Research and Social Issues.* New York: Holt, Rinehart & Winston, 1976.

Peck, R. F., and Havighurst, R. J. *The Psychology of Character Development.* New York: Wiley, 1960.

Piaget, J. *The Moral Judgment of the Child.* London: Routledge & Kegan Paul, 1932.

Piaget, J. *The Psychology of Intelligence.* Totowa, N.J.: Littlefield Adams, 1947.

Piaget, J. *Psychology and Epistemology.* New York: Viking Press, 1970.

Power, C. "The Just Community Approach to Moral Education." *Journal of Moral Education,* 1988, *17,* 195-208.

Selman, R. L. *The Growth of Interpersonal Understanding: Development and Clinical Analysis.* New York: Academic Press, 1980.

Selman, R. L. "The Development of Interpersonal Competence: The Role of Understanding in Conduct." *Developmental Review,* 1981, *1,* 401-422.

Smetana, J. G. *Concepts of Self and Morality: Women's Reasoning About Abortion.* New York: Praeger, 1982.

Turiel, E. *The Development of Social Knowledge: Morality and Convention.* Cambridge, England: Cambridge University Press, 1983.

Turiel, E., Killen, M., and Helwig, C. "Morality: Its Structure, Functions, and Vagaries." In J. Kagan and S. Lamb (eds.), *The Emergence of Moral Concepts in Young Children.* Chicago: University of Chicago Press, 1987.

Turiel, E., and Smetana, J. G. "Social Knowledge and Action: The Coordination of Domains." In W. M. Kurtines and J. L. Gewirtz (eds.), *Morality, Moral Behavior and Moral Development: Basic Issues in Theory and Research.* New York: Wiley, 1984.

Turiel, E., Smetana, J. G., and Killen, M. "Social Contexts in Social Cognitive Development." In W. M. Kurtines and J. L. Gewirtz (eds.), *Handbook of Moral Behavior and Development.* Vol. 2: *Research.* Hillsdale, N.J.: Erlbaum, in press.

Elliot Turiel is professor of Education at the University of California, Berkeley. He is author of The Development of Social Knowledge: Morality and Convention *(1983) and continues to conduct research on moral reasoning and action.*

The motivation to act morally is a result of moral reasoning and understanding.

Kohlberg's Theory and Moral Motivation

Augusto Blasi

One of the most interesting and potentially most revolutionary implications of Kohlberg's theory of moral development concerns moral motivation. This may seem paradoxical, since moral motivation was not a main focus of Kohlberg's thinking and, in fact, is one of those aspects for which his theory is frequently and severely criticized.

Criticism comes in two forms: it is claimed either that Kohlberg has no theory of moral motivation or that his views on this issue are radically inadequate. Considering that morality is ultimately oriented to action, both forms of criticism imply a condemnation of the theory as a whole.

Concerning the first criticism, it is easy to show that Kohlberg did in fact address the issue of motivation and that his theory revolves around one central proposition: moral understanding is the basis for the motive to act morally. Whether or not this proposition is adequate is largely an empirical question that so far has been left untested. This chapter addresses a different question: how should moral motivation be understood from a Kohlbergian perspective, that is, from a perspective that accepts understanding as the essential basis of morality?

Kohlberg's Views on Moral Motivation

A frequently reprinted table summarizing Kohlberg's six stages of moral development (for example, Kohlberg, 1976) has been used as the source of his ideas on moral motivation. In it, under the heading "Reasons for Doing Right," Kohlberg listed the reasons for acting morally that are characteristic of each stage: "avoidance and punishment" at Stage 1; "to serve one's needs and interests" at Stage 2; "the need to be a good person in your own eyes and those of others" at Stage 3; and so on.

What Kohlberg meant by "reason" in this context is not entirely clear, since he did not explicitly define the term in either the table or the text. Frequently, these reasons have been taken as motives for action; thus Kohlberg has been interpreted as suggesting that each moral stage is marked by the decline of certain motives and the ascension of others. This interpretation guided the two empirical studies that focused directly on moral motivation: Schwartz, Feldman, Brown, and Heingartner (1969) and Percival (1979). In the latter, for instance, the investigator hypothesized and found that people at Kohlberg's Stage 3 perform better on a learning task when the incentives consist of interpersonal approval, whereas Stage 4 individuals do better when the incentives are related to distributive equality and to the expectations of an authority.

This motivational interpretation has also been the source of critical reactions. Pritchard (1984), for instance, read the list of stage-related reasons as a sequence of motivational patterns and criticized Kohlberg for postulating a sudden, unprepared shift from the essentially egoistical motivation of the preconventional level to the altruistic motivation of Stage 3.

Kohlberg, however, explicitly, though not always clearly, viewed these responses to his work as misinterpretations and warned readers against a motivational understanding of the stages. These, he stated, "represent something more general than motives. Obviously, even post-conventional people are concerned about approval and conventional people have some inner moral motives" (Kohlberg, 1974, p. 17). The same idea is repeated in one of his more recent publications: "Many readers of my earlier writings . . . were left with the belief that my moral stages were eventually expressions of a developmental hierarchy of motives. . . . In fact, however, I have avoided this emotivist view of the moral stage" (Kohlberg, 1986, p. 498). Avoiding punishment, satisfying one's needs, or caring for others should be seen, instead, as reasons in a logical argument, that is, as criteria by which people at different stages understand which actions are morally right.

Of course, this nonmotivational view is the only one that is compatible with Kohlberg's cognitive structural presuppositions: moral stages are considered to be "hard" and are contrasted with the "soft" stages described by Loevinger or Gilligan, precisely because they are based on a rigorously coherent logic, without any admixture of psychological motives and feelings (Kohlberg, Levine, and Hewer, 1983).

Kohlberg seems to have understood the relationship between psychological motives and structured reasons in the following way: Some basic social motives, including empathy and the need for social interaction and acceptance, may be present from very early in life. These motives remain active throughout an individual's life but are progressively transformed through cognitive and ego development. However, they acquire moral meaning only when they are integrated with moral understanding. Morally, therefore, what changes from stage to stage are not the motives but rather their evaluation and selection on the basis of moral reasons.

In sum, Kohlberg did not confuse reasons and motives, as some have claimed (for example, Straughan, 1986). Rather, he attributed motivational power to reason and argued that moral reasons have their own independent motives for moral action. This point deserves some elaboration. From Kohlberg's perspective, it would be incorrect to postulate that the power to determine action lies with psychological motives and that moral reasons simply give a new meaning to preexisting motives. In fact, moral understanding must be able to guide and control these motives. For instance, such understanding must be effective in controlling the natural human desire for social acceptance, when it produces actions that one judges to be immoral; they lead to solutions that foster the interests of only some people and therefore are unfair overall.

This is precisely the point that many critics cannot accept. One can find two general kinds of argument for divorcing cognition and motivation. The first is philosophical in nature and points to the purely descriptive nature of knowledge. The second argument is based on the very common experience that there is a gap between having a valid and good reason to engage in a certain action and actually engaging in that action. The fact that this experience is shared by many of us makes this argument very powerful and difficult to dismiss.

Kohlberg was sensitive to this problem and tried to address it in his later work (Kohlberg and Candee, 1984a, 1984b). Without going into the details of his solutions, they all seem to share one main idea: certain kinds of reasoning yield better reasons, and better reasons are more likely to lead to moral action. Needless to say, an attempt to remedy through cognition what seems to be intrinsic limitations of cognition cannot be very persuasive.

To briefly summarize the main points of this section, Kohlberg was fully aware that for a cognitive theory of morality to be viable, reasons must have motivating power; to the extent that morality is, at the core, a matter of evaluation and justification, the motivation to act morally must proceed from moral understanding. And yet, from the perspective of motivation and action, understanding and reasoning have obvious limitations, which cannot be overcome by more and better understanding and reasoning. Something else, then, is necessary to link reasons to motivation and action. We need a psychological theory to explain how and why moral understanding leads, when it does so, to the desire to act morally.

Emotions as the Source of Moral Motivation

One possible solution, consistently resisted by Kohlberg, would be to resort to emotions. There are two general arguments for associating emotions with morality. One is that emotions define or at least partially constitute the moral phenomenon (Rich, 1986). The second argument, and the exclusive focus here, is that emotions, because of their intrinsic motivational power, are necessary to vitalize a rather inert cognition and to actually produce moral action.

This view has a long and venerable history both in philosophy and in psychology. Particularly influential has been Hume's (1978) opinion that practical reasoning, including moral reasoning, consists of grafting factual beliefs on certain "passions," which then function as basic premises. In spite of its authority, this view is unconvincing for several reasons. One is that emotions (if one were to understand Hume's passions as emotions), even the most complex ones, are still subject to evaluation from moral or other perspectives. Another and related reason is that emotions may or may not be integrated in one's personality: namely, they may be experienced as external and alien or may be accepted and identified as belonging to one's inner self.

But the important point in this context is that emotions cannot accomplish by themselves the job of functioning as motivational springs. The older term, passion, and the more recent term, affect, are ambiguous in meaning and comprise two seemingly different sets of processes. Included in the first set are fear, joy, sadness, anxiety, empathy, pride, guilt, and so on, all of which can be considered emotions in a narrow sense. The second set includes needs, drives, impulses, whims, desires, and commitments. These processes, whether conscious or unconscious, are strictly motivational and are defined by their capacity to direct action toward certain goals.

These two sets of processes, emotions and motivations, are conceptually and psychologically different, even if concretely they are related to each other. As such, emotions do not have motivational power, and vice versa, motives are not intrinsically emotional. For instance, feeling sad does not implicate any movement toward a certain goal; the same is true of more active emotions such as joy or pride. By contrast, a process like determination does not necessarily involve a specific emotional experience (even though its subsequent frustration does). Instead, it seems to be characterized by a purposeful orientation of the person as a whole. The same is true of such constructs as commitment, obligation, duty, and responsibility, even when these terms are preceded by "sense of." These constructs are indeed relevant to moral motivation, not because of an emotive experience, which may be largely absent, but because they indicate an investment of the person in moral goals.

If this analysis is correct, then the connection between emotion and motivation cannot be taken for granted but must be accounted for in psychological terms. In other words, one needs a psychological theory to functionally relate emotions to moral motivation and action *for exactly the same reasons* that one needs a theory to functionally relate moral understanding and moral motivation.

In psychology, a theory that ties motivation to emotion exists and has been very influential, namely, tension-reduction theory. Even though this theory has traditionally been elaborated in connection with anxiety, in recent years it has been used by Hoffman (1978, 1982) to explain how empathic and guilt feelings lead to altruistic behavior. In Hoffman's view, empathy and guilt lead to altruism, but only indirectly, through the tension produced by these emotions and through the association between the effects of altruism and the relief of tension.

Hoffman's theory is more complex and more differentiated than this brief summary can suggest. Even so, it underscores and exemplifies the need for a psychological model that ties emotions to moral action. Only this kind of model can help us to address the important question of whether an emotive account is compatible with what we otherwise know of moral motivation and morality in general. The model proposed by Hoffman, for instance, has been criticized for distorting the other-oriented nature of empathy and altruism (Batson, Fultz, and Schoenrade, 1987). From the perspective of cognitive developmentalism, this explanation does not sufficiently preserve what seem to be two necessary aspects of morality: the justification of the action and the freedom to choose whether to act or not according to one's judgment.

Moral Motivation as a Result of Integration

If, as I believe, it is essential for morality to remain centered in reason and knowledge and to have these processes protected from distorting interferences; and if, in contrast, reason and knowledge do not have the power to motivate action, then the solution must consist of making reason itself, knowledge, and understanding the object of one's motives and desires. In a discussion of Kohlberg's theory, Bailey (1986, p. 205) indicated the same solution: "It seems necessary to posit some kind of affective commitment *to* reason, *to* the results of one's cognition . . . ; care for reason, a sense of obligation to one's own reasoning, seems to be the necessary mainspring which drives Kohlberg's whole system."

In light of the distinction between emotions and motivations advanced earlier, the processes Bailey (1986) refers to—commitment, sense of obligation, and care, to which one could add responsibility and sense of integrity and personal consistency—are not emotions in the strict sense but rather motivational processes. All of these processes should be considered as a direct result, and as indications, of the integration of reason and moral understanding in one's personality and sense of self. Emotions can be the by-product of this integration.

Psychologists of various theoretical persuasions, even those who perceive its importance, do not seem to understand too well what this type of integration involves and how it is accomplished. In a general sense, it consists of making moral beliefs and values, and also moral emotions, our own, our possession; placing them next to our other desires, interests, and aspirations and determining their rank in our motivational hierarchy; investing in them our attention and effort; and building on them our most intimate sense of ourselves, what we think we deeply and truly are.

Kohlberg did not look at moral motivation in these terms. In his early work (for example, Kohlberg, 1963, 1964, 1969), he discussed the psychoanalytic and the learning theory concepts of internalization, which represented the then-dominant views concerning the integration of morality in personality. He rejected both of them as incompatible with a cognitive view of morality and moral development. Kohlberg well understood that in these theories internalized morality remains external to the person, essentially because neither theory can acknowledge the real and necessary integrating function that knowledge and understanding have for personality.

But Kohlberg seems to have believed that cognition constitutes the only kind of personal integration, or that other and deeper types of integration automatically flow out of understanding and follow the same processes. This limitation of his theory can be easily accepted, once we realize, as suggested earlier, that contemporary psychology does not even have a differentiated language to deal with moral integration.

And herein lies the potentially revolutionary value for psychology of Kohlberg's view of moral motivation: His uncompromising insistence that morality must be based on reason and understanding forces us to look at these problems in ways that are radically different from familiar psychological modes of thinking.

References

Bailey, C. "Kohlberg on Morality and Feeling." In S. Modgil and C. Modgil (eds.), *Lawrence Kohlberg: Consensus and Controversy.* London: Falmer Press, 1986.

Batson, C. D., Fultz, J., and Schoenrade, P. A. "Distress and Empathy: Two Qualitatively Distinct Vicarious Emotions with Different Motivational Consequences." *Journal of Personality,* 1987, 55, 19–39.

Hoffman, M. L. "Empathy, Its Development and Prosocial Implications." In C. B. Keasey (ed.), *1977 Nebraska Symposium on Motivation.* Lincoln: University of Nebraska Press, 1978.

Hoffman, M. L. "Development of Prosocial Motivation: Empathy and Guilt." In N. Eisenberg (ed.), *The Development of Prosocial Behavior.* New York: Academic Press, 1982.

Hume, D. *A Treatise of Human Nature.* (2nd ed.) L. A. Selby-Bigge (ed.). Oxford, England: Oxford University Press, 1978. (Originally published 1739-1740.)

Kohlberg, L. "Moral Development and Identification." In H. Stevenson (ed.), *Child Psychology, 62nd Yearbook of the National Society for the Study of Education.* Chicago: University of Chicago Press, 1963.

Kohlberg, L. "Development of Moral Character and Moral Ideology." In M. L. Hoffman and L. W. Hoffman (eds.), *Review of Child Development Research.* Vol. 1. New York: Russell Sage Foundation, 1964.

Kohlberg, L. "Stage and Sequence: The Cognitive-Developmental Approach to Socialization." In D. A. Goslin (ed.), *Handbook of Socialization Theory and Research.* Chicago: Rand McNally, 1969.

Kohlberg, L. "Six Stages of Moral Judgment." Unpublished manuscript, Harvard University, Graduate School of Education, Moral Education Research Foundation, 1974.

Kohlberg, L. "Moral Stages and Moralization: The Cognitive-Developmental Approach." In T. Lickona (ed.), *Moral Development: Theory, Research, and Social Issues.* New York: Holt, Rinehart & Winston, 1976.

Kohlberg, L. "A Current Statement on Some Theoretical Issues." In S. Modgil and C. Modgil (eds.), *Lawrence Kohlberg: Consensus and Controversy.* London: Falmer Press, 1986.

Kohlberg, L., and Candee, D. "The Relationship of Moral Judgment to Moral Action." In L. Kohlberg, *Essays on Moral Development.* Vol. 2: *The Psychology of Moral Development.* New York: Harper & Row, 1984a.

Kohlberg, L., and Candee, D. "The Relationship of Moral Judgment to Moral Action." In W. M. Kurtines and J. L. Gewirtz (eds.), *Morality, Moral Behavior, and Moral Development.* New York: Wiley, 1984b.

Kohlberg, L., Levine, C., and Hewer, A. *Moral Stages: A Current Formulation and a Response to Critics.* New York: Karger, 1983.

Percival, T. Q. "Cognitive and Motivational Parallels in Moral Development." *Canadian Journal of Behavioral Science,* 1979, *11,* 214-224.

Pritchard, M. S. "Cognition and Affect in Moral Development: A Critique of Lawrence Kohlberg." *Journal of Value Inquiry,* 1984, *18,* 35-49.

Rich, J. M. "Morality, Reason and Emotion." In S. Modgil and C. Modgil (eds.), *Lawrence Kohlberg: Consensus and Controversy.* London: Falmer Press, 1986.

Schwartz, S. H., Feldman, K. A., Brown, M. E., and Heingartner, A. "Some Personality Correlates of Conduct in Two Situations of Moral Conflict." *Journal of Personality,* 1969, *37,* 41-57.

Straughan, R. "Why Act on Kohlberg's Moral Judgments? (Or How to Reach Stage 6 and Remain a Bastard)." In S. Modgil and C. Modgil (eds.), *Lawrence Kohlberg: Consensus and Controversy.* London: Falmer Press, 1986.

Augusto Blasi is professor of psychology at the University of Massachusetts, Boston and is presently working on the issue of the development of the self and identity and their relation to morality.

Attention to particular aspects of persons, contexts, and emotions is an essential aspect of morality.

Universality and Particularity

Lawrence Blum

I am honored to contribute to this volume on Lawrence Kohlberg's work. Kohlberg was always an inspirational figure for me—first, as a psychologist who saw both philosophy and psychology as necessary for an understanding of the phenomena of morality and moral development; and second, as a thinker who invited criticism of his views and who struggled to come to grips with the criticism. As a philosophical critic of Kohlberg's view of morality, I always felt welcome to engage him in dialogue.

Complementary Principles of Morality

The notion of universality plays various roles within Kohlberg's system. First, it is involved in the empirical claim that the development from preconventional through conventional to principled reasoning is a human and cultural universal (though according to Kohlberg's own findings only a minority of people in any culture actually attain the highest stage). Universality is also involved in the related normative claim that, from a universal standpoint, the empirically final stage of moral reasoning, preferred by all of those who can understand that stage, is also the normatively most adequate form of moral reasoning.

Without directly taking issue with either of these claims, I focus on a third claim concerning how, for Kohlberg, universality characterizes

---

I have benefited in writing this paper from an unpublished manuscript by Peter Davson-Galle, "Against 'Moral' Partialism," Department of Philosophy, Tasmanian State Institute of Technology, Laurceston, Australia. I also thank Owen Flanagan, Jr., and David Wong for helpful comments on early drafts of this chapter and Johannah Meehan for insights into Habermas's recent views.

the nature of morality itself at the sixth and highest stage of development. Specifically, the universality of the highest stage contrasts with the conventional and relative stance of the agent at the conventional stages. At the lower stages the person either restricts the domain of moral principle to a particular social entity, whether a particular role conception or an entire society, or else he or she uses a thus-restricted moral conception as if it had universal validity. In either case the conventional reasoner's moral conception lacks true universality.

By contrast, for the highest-stage moral individual, moral principles are necessarily universal. They define a standpoint beyond any particular society, from which the specific morality of a society can be evaluated. This characterization applies to Kohlberg's (1958) original description of his sixth stage, as characterized by principles of equality, universal rights, and justice. But it also applies to the 1984 revision in which the sixth stage is characterized formally rather than in terms of a particular content. What this formal characterization guarantees is that whatever principles the individual holds, these principles must be universal in form and scope; they must be applicable to all persons.

I suggest that while Kohlberg (and Jürgen Habermas, who agrees with him on this point) may be right in seeing a link between mature moral reasoning and universality so understood, there is also an important incompleteness in a conception of morality that defines it (in its highest form) exclusively in terms of universality. One can see this incompleteness by examining two contrasts, each involving universality. One is the contrast between universality and conventionalism or parochialism; the other, between universality and particularity.

The contrast between universality and conventionalism may be between a more and a less adequate or developed moral outlook. Leaving aside the concerns about cultural bias and relativity raised by Schweder, Mahapatra, and Miller (1987), at least in Western cultures I believe that we rightly regard an appreciation of the equal and inherent dignity of all persons and a belief that all human beings have rights and deserve justice as moral advances over less comprehensive—and, in that way, more parochial—moralities.

However, the second contrast, between universality and particularity, marks a tension between two equally essential components of any adequate conception of morality. Reasoning in terms of universal principles is not the only moral capacity constituting someone as morally mature, as a person possessing morally good traits of character. Universal principles do not by themselves characterize lived moral agency. To possess moral traits of character involves something more, namely, particularity. Particularity, as I understand it, is knowledge of the moral character of the particular situation facing a moral agent at a particular time. To speak of particularity as a general moral capacity is to refer to a moral agent's general ability to know the moral character of situations she faces.

Particularity is not only knowledge that certain features given in the description of a situation are morally relevant features (features that need to be taken into account in moral action). Particularity presupposes such knowledge and goes beyond it. For it involves getting the description of the situation one is faced with right in the first place. For example, it involves seeing that a situation does involve lying, dishonor, and cruelty in the first place.

Particularity is a complex phenomenon; it is not a unitary ability. I focus here on one element in particularity, namely, the ability and disposition to understand other specific persons in their individuality, and to be aware of what is going on with them in concrete situations. This involves, for example, knowing or perceiving when a specific person is in need, being cruelly treated, or in danger of having her dignity attacked.

One way to state the contrast between universal principle and particularity is that between seeing others in light of the commonality that makes all persons appropriate objects of universal, rational principles, and seeing them in light of each one's specific individuality. These ways of viewing are complementary, but both are necessary in the fully morally developed individual. A person who holds and reasons in terms of all of the correct universal principles of dignity and justice, but who does not recognize when others are in need, when their dignity is in danger, or when they are being treated unjustly, would not be a fully morally developed person, though she might be an advanced moral reasoner.

The recognition of need in others is often not a simple matter. Habermas reminds us in his writings of the necessity of what he calls "need interpretation." In the context of everyday life, other persons do not just present themselves with their needs displayed and articulated for us to respond to. Rather, recognizing and acknowledging that someone is in need is a task that is itself both cognitive and moral. Suppose, to take a mundane example, I am riding on the subway; another passenger not far from me is holding several packages. In the rush of everyday life, many of her fellow passengers might see her only as someone carrying packages. But it may well be that attention to this particular person reveals that she is struggling with these packages, that she is quite uncomfortable standing the way she is, and that the seated passengers near her could help her in various ways, say, by standing up and allowing her to sit down, or by offering to hold some of the packages. That is, this woman's need can be "seen" and "taken in"; or, on the contrary, it can go unrecognized, unacknowledged, and thus unresponded to.

The recognition of need—and, more generally, the understanding of particular persons in particular situations—is an essential capacity of a morally mature individual. Without it, moral agency, no matter how developed and sophisticated the moral reasoning that informs it, can accomplish little. Moreover, this attentiveness to and understanding of others in their particularity is normally an expression of a person's caring about others. It is care that renders the agent open and receptive to seeing the other's need.

This caring understanding of others is not always easy to achieve. As in the subway example, self-absorption and lack of other-directed awareness can prevent one from seeing that another person is being treated cruelly, is depressed, or has been emotionally wounded by an insensitive remark. And within the context of personal relations, our own desires and needs for particular other persons, and our self-centered or insufficiently caring investment in a certain view of that person, can block from our vision the other's true needs.

Because the moral capacities involved in particularity are not focused on universality and universal principle, one might be tempted to confuse particularity with less than Stage 6 reasoning. But particularity has little to do with conventional reasoning or social contract. The ability to know others in their particularity, that is, to be attentive to the situations of others in order to discern their needs, depends in its fullest realization on a secure sense of one's own self. The nonautonomous or not-yet-autonomous self will see others' needs too much through the prism of her own needs; she will not grasp the other in his otherness. So this particularistic moral capacity can be seen to require an autonomous self, a self that Kohlberg rightly saw as also being a necessary condition for principled, postconventional reasoning.

Kohlberg on Particularity and Morality

In his second volume of *Essays on Moral Development,* Kohlberg (1984) seemed to acknowledge that his previous definition of morality as comprising the domain of universal principles of justice and dignity was incomplete (pp. 227, 229, 307). He struggled to incorporate within the framework of his own theory some appreciation of particularity. He makes several suggestions in this direction, most of which conflict with one another, and none of which taken alone is adequate.

Kohlberg suggests (here termed view 1) that the nonjustice part of morality be seen in terms of the claims of special, personal relationships, such as family or friendships (1984, pp. 228, 231–232). It is true that the domain of personal relationships has not been given its full due in the rationalist and universalist tradition within which Kohlberg worked, and Kohlberg's acknowledgment of that domain is welcome. Nevertheless, he is not consistent in the importance he accords to it. At another point (view 2), he appears to give personal relations a kind of equal status with the more public domain of universal principles (p. 228). At still another point (view 3), he sees it as secondary or merely supplementary to the domain of justice (p. 229). In addition Kohlberg approvingly cites Gertrud Nunner-Winkler, who takes yet a fourth position (view 4) that the domain of personal relationships be seen as part of the ideals of the "good life" rather than of morality, properly so-called (p. 360). Views 2 and 3 contrast with view 4 in acknowledging that personal relations are genuinely a part of morality itself.

Kohlberg also suggests (view 5) that ultimately the domain of special relationships can itself be handled, or encompassed, by a morality of justice and universal principles (1984, p. 228). His view here is not merely that the domain of personal relationships contains a confluence or interaction of two distinct types of moral notions (for example, justice and care) but also that justice and universal principles are by themselves sufficient to capture whatever is of moral significance in the domain of personal relationships.

According to view 5, we find out how to act morally in our personal relationships by consulting universal principles of justice, or principles derived from them. This seems to deny what the other four views assert, namely, that there is something genuinely distinctive about the domain of personal relationships with respect to the domain encompassed by universal principles (1984, p. 228). View 1 says the domains are distinct, view 2 that they are distinct but equally significant, view 3 that they are distinct but justice is the more fundamental domain, and view 4 that personal relations have to do with the good life, not with morality. So Kohlberg's five views are by no means compatible with one another. And it is probably fair to say that Kohlberg had not entirely decided on how to think about the domain of personal relationships from a moral point of view.

In any case, four of Kohlberg's five views are not adequate to handle what is involved in particularity more generally. Regarding view 4, there is no basis for excluding personal relations from the domain of morality proper. As Kohlberg comes close to acknowledging (1984, pp. 229, 343, 370), we do have duties to our children, spouses, and, perhaps, friends. Certain requirements govern these relationships (though such requirements constitute only one aspect of the relationships). In the passage about a woman contemplating divorce, Kohlberg seems to agree that certain moral principles do govern family life, such as the "principle of family unity" and the "principle of the welfare of the child" (Kohlberg, 1984, p. 230).

Hence, while there might be value in distinguishing between the right and the good, or between moral requirement and personal ideal, these distinctions do not correspond to the distinction between a universalistic public morality and morality in personal relations. The former distinctions will have to be drawn within personal relations, and perhaps within the public domain as well.

For similar reasons, view 3—that personal relations are less significant a domain of morality than the public domain of justice—is also incorrect. No grounds are given by Kohlberg for regarding the private domain as any less important to the moral life than the public domain. Ordinarily, we do regard both domains as reflecting significantly on an individual's moral character. View 5—that there is *no* significant moral difference between the two domains—is thus incorrect as well. While the differences may be only of degree, the moral notions of care, attention, personal commitment, and responsibility play a greater role in the arena of personal relations than in the arena of public action (Kohlberg, 1984, p. 228).

Furthermore, all five of Kohlberg's views presuppose that particularity is coextensive with the domain of personal relationships. But the example of the subway rider mentioned earlier suggests otherwise. Our capacity to attend to individual others applies not only to the morality of personal relationships—although this is a very important realm of its operation—but also to relationships with strangers, as well as to intermediate cases such as professional-to-client relationships (see Blum, 1990; Noddings, 1984). We can say, provisionally, that particularity encompasses any encounter of one person with another. The Judeo-Christian conception of the neighbor seems well-suited to capture this element of particularity beyond the arena of strictly personal relationships, by emphasizing an encounter with a particular other.

Kohlberg makes yet a sixth suggestion (view 6) about how particularity might be encompassed within his own framework for morality: rationalist moral theories such as his own and Kant's (except for the rigoristic and absolutistic strands in Kant) have always taken particularity into account, in that general principles have always been understood to encompass their applicability to particular circumstances (Kohlberg, 1984, p. 359). That is, rationalist moral theory has always understood that every general principle in its application to particular circumstances, by virtue of taking such context into account, is recognized to have exceptions (Kohlberg, 1982).

This rationalist view is misleading, however. First, it cannot be assumed that the process by which we recognize that moral rules have exceptions is anything like the process by which we arrive at rational and universal principles in the first place. The rationalistic process by which a moral person arrives at universal moral principles such as justice, equal rights, and the human dignity of all persons is typically quite different from the way that a moral person recognizes exceptions to a given moral rule. The recognition of exceptions typically comes in a confrontation with a particular situation, evoking an awareness, grounded in a particularistic understanding of the situation, that the rule in question does not apply there. This is to say that the acknowledgment of actual exceptions to rules involves a complex negotiation between the stance of universality and the stance of particularity. Thus, the recognition of the significance of context cannot be taken as support for the view that universality already encompasses, or accounts for, particularity, as view 6 implies.

Moreover, even when a moral agent possesses a universalized rule (whether containing exceptions or not), there is still a gap between the principle and its application to a particular situation. Kohlberg's view fails to recognize that the particularity involved in *applying* the rule involves a very different sort of capacity from that which is involved in *formulating* the universal principle in the first place. An understanding of individuals in their specific situations requires a different sort of capacity than that needed to recognize and formulate universal principles (though, as argued earlier, the formulation of principles with a lot of exceptions often involves an interaction of both particularity and universality). It is not a simple or quasi-mechanical matter to apply a principle in a situation, as Kohlberg's view here implies. Rather, rule application often involves complex perceptiveness, attentiveness, and understanding of situations and individuals.

The capacity for forming universal principles is a much more self-reflective and intellectualized capacity than that for particularity. Particularity, while cognitive, is more bound up with our emotional natures. Indeed, the grounding of particularistic care in emotion is trivialized by characterizations such as "affectively tinged" ideas (Kohlberg, 1984, p. 228), which presume that if the "tinge" were removed, we would be left with only rational, universal principles and their derivatives. If particularity in its form of understanding of individuals is at least partly dependent on caring, then because caring is both emotional and cognitive, the dependence of particularity on emotion is evident. Particularity is also less dependent on its own articulatability than is principled reasoning. If I act according to an autonomously generated moral principle, then I know that I have done so and am able to say what that principle is. But to the extent that my action is based on a particularistic understanding of my situation, I might have such an understanding without either recognizing that I have it, knowing how I arrived at it, or being able to articulate it (see Blum, 1988).

Habermas appears to agree with this criticism of Kohlberg. However, what Habermas sees as bridging the gap between universal principle and particular application is different from what I mean by particularity.

It may seem that I have not yet shown that particularity is part of a person's distinct moral makeup. But this analytic gap is apparent only if one identifies morality with nothing more than the intellectual generation of universal principles. My assumption has been that even if one accepts for the moment a central role for universal principles in the moral life, an individual whom we would regard as morally mature or morally developed would still have to do more than know how to arrive at, or reason to, moral principles. She would also have to live according to those principles. And what I am arguing here is that to live according to those principles requires particularity—the understanding of particular situations, which in turn involves (in part) caring attentiveness to individual persons.

In this way I have argued that particularity is no less important to morality than universality. It is not that particularity is a nonmoral, merely psychological capacity instrumental to the correct application of moral principles to particular situations. It would be no less true to say that reasoning to valid moral principles is instrumental to their application to particular situations. The point is rather that what is being called "application of moral principles" as if it were a mere appendage to a purely rationalistic or universalist formulation of morality, is no less than a critical part of what is involved in living a moral life. And living a moral life requires, equally, both universality and particularity. (Because of space limitations, the argument developed here does not challenge the assumption that all moral action is based on universal, rational principles. This assumption is challenged in Blum [1986, 1987], where I argue that non-principle-based, situation-specific caring can motivate morally good actions.)

Let me turn to a brief consideration of Jürgen Habermas's partial criticism of Kohlberg's views and his further development of Kohlberg's basic approach toward an ethic based in dialogue and communication. Habermas (1979) sees Kohlberg as having provided the basic universalistic and rational framework within which morality should be understood. But he criticizes Kohlberg's claim that Stage 6 is the highest stage of development because he sees that stage as purely "monologic" (1979, p. 90). That is, for Kohlberg, at Stage 6 the individual moral agent generates the highest principles from a (universalization) procedure that she engages in by herself. For Habermas, by contrast, the highest stage (Stage 7) involves actual dialogue with particular others about moral principles to be agreed on. Habermas sees principles of dialogue as bridging the gap mentioned earlier between pure universality and its application to particular circumstances.

This important corrective of Kohlberg's view is a step toward the particularity I have been arguing for here. Kohlberg (1984) replies to Habermas's (1979) criticism in two ways. First, he says that his description of Stage 6 is entirely "consistent with" Habermas's principle of dialogue. For example, Kohlberg argues that Stage 6 involves "ideal role taking" (1984, p. 385), which is consistent with Habermas's dialogic approach, since engaging in dialogue is a good way to learn about the perspectives of other persons. But to argue that Stage 7 is compatible with Stage 6 is an insufficient answer to Habermas's criticism. It is no doubt true that engaging in actual dialogue with the persons to be affected by one's action is compatible with imagining oneself in the situations of those persons, insofar as the results of the latter method may, on particular occasions, coincide with the results of the former. But Habermas's point is that engaging in actual dialogue is superior as a general method for accomplishing the universalization, that is, the taking of everyone's perspective into account, required by the highest stage of morality. In short, the dialogic or interactional method is superior to the monologic achievement of that universalization.

Second, Kohlberg takes this stronger position that dialogue is actually the best way to achieve what is stated in Stage 6 (1984, p. 386). Yet, if Kohlberg is saying that the dialogic method is actually superior to the monologic method as a way of engaging in ideal role taking, then he seems to have conceded Habermas's point, at least in regard to the way that Stage 6 has generally been understood and conveyed in Kohlberg's writings.

Kohlberg's failure to show that Habermas's interactional approach is not superior to the more Kantian-monological approach, which Stage 6 has generally been thought to embody, is not meant to preclude the possibility that Kohlberg was moving toward a more interactional and less individualistic and rationalist understanding of morality. The likelihood of this shift is suggested by his work on just community schools, as detailed in Power, Higgins, and Kohlberg (1989).

Habermas's dialogic view of morality sees the phenomenon as more social and less individualistic, and as more concrete and grounded and less abstract, than Kohlberg's view. Yet, I do not think that Habermas's dialogic Stage 7 succeeds in incorporating all of what I have meant by particularity. Habermas sees the dialogic process as involving different persons who seek grounds for agreement with others about moral principles. In this way Habermas follows the logic of Kohlberg's position, giving a social (but not conventional) form to the search for rational principles that is inherent in the logic of Kohlberg's stages.

But not all interpersonal events of moral significance involve a search for agreement or even a dialogue of any sort. Some involve the attempt by a moral agent to understand what the other person is about outside a context of seeking moral agreement, or when the other is not necessarily trying to communicate with that agent. In reaching that understanding the moral agent has to attend to more than the explicit truth-claiming and agreement-seeking aspects of speech. In fact, people's own needs are often masked by their explicit speech, a point that Habermas makes elsewhere. And understanding the needs of another—an important task of particularity—involves attention to other cues about a person, for example, her situation, bodily comportment, and emotional expression (see Young, 1987, on which the present criticism of Habermas is based). Hence the kind of interaction with others that produces particularistic understanding—rooted in the emotions—of persons does not necessarily take the form of an agreement-seeking dialogue about moral principles, which Habermas (1979) sees as the highest stage of morality and which he suggests provides the principles of application of universal morality to concrete situations.

Furthermore, the kind of understanding of others involved in particularity often takes place outside of speech situations altogether, as illustrated by my earlier example of the woman in the subway. More generally, particular understanding does not always require interaction or stem from interaction, though Habermas is right to be generally suspicious of any purely monologic moral efforts—whether of noninteractional understanding or of generation of principle.

Conclusion

In fact, no principles of application, no matter how they are generated, could provide all of what I have called particularity. For, as I have argued, no matter how detailed the principles that one applies, the agent must first perceive the moral character of the situation at hand in order to begin drawing on the appropriate principles. No principles can ensure the accuracy of those particular perceptions.

How the particularistic dimension of morality relates to the universal dimension that Kohlberg explored is a necessary and fruitful area in the study of the moral domain. Lawrence Kohlberg's own self-critical combination of philosophy and psychology well serves as a salutary model for the interdisciplinary pursuit of such an inquiry.

References

Blum, L. "Iris Murdoch and the Domain of the Moral." *Philosophical Studies,* 1986, *50,* 343-367.

Blum, L. "Particularity and Responsiveness." In J. Kagan and S. Lamb (eds.), *The Emergence of Morality in Young Children.* Chicago: University of Chicago Press, 1987.

Blum, L. "Gilligan and Kohlberg: Implications for Moral Theory." *Ethics,* 1988, *98,* 472-491.

Blum, L. "Vocation, Friendship, and Community: Limitations of the Personal-Impersonal Framework." In O. Flanagan, Jr., and A. Rorty (eds.), *Psychology and Morality.* Cambridge, Mass.: MIT Press, 1990.

Habermas, J. "Moral Development and Ego Identity." In *Communication and the Evolution of Society.* Boston: Beacon Press, 1979.

Kohlberg, L. "The Development of Modes of Moral Thinking and Choice in the Years 10 to 16." Unpublished doctoral dissertation, University of Chicago, 1958.

Kohlberg, L. "Reply to Owen Flanagan." *Ethics,* 1982, *92,* 513-528.

Kohlberg, L. *Essays on Moral Development.* Vol. 2: *The Psychology of Moral Development.* San Francisco: Harper & Row, 1984.

Noddings, N. *Caring: A Feminine Approach to Ethics and Moral Education.* Berkeley and Los Angeles: University of California Press, 1984.

Power, F. C., Higgins, A., and Kohlberg, L. *Lawrence Kohlberg's Approach to Moral Education.* New York: Columbia University Press, 1989.

Schweder, R., Mahapatra, M., and Miller, J. "Culture and Moral Development." In J. Kagan and S. Lamb (eds.), *The Emergence of Morality in Young Children.* Chicago: University of Chicago Press, 1987.

Young, I. "Impartiality and the Civic Public: Some Implications of Feminist Critiques of Moral and Political Theory." In S. Benhabib and D. Cornell (eds.), *Feminism as Critique.* Minneapolis: University of Minnesota Press, 1987.

Lawrence Blum is professor of philosophy at the University of Massachusetts, Boston. His interest areas are moral theory, moral education, and moral psychology.

Some themes from Kohlberg's work are given life through a story from a third-grade classroom.

A Story for Larry

Eleanor Duckworth with Joanne Cleary

To my regret I never did work with Larry Kohlberg. I realize that, in parallel, we faced many similar educational issues. He showed great interest in the work of a group of teachers that I was associated with under the umbrella of the Cambridge Commission for Nuclear Disarmament and Peace Education. He liked their stories. Joanne Cleary was a member of that group, and these remarks consist essentially of a recent story from her classroom, which I think he also would have liked.

To set the context for the story, I refer the reader to a number of thoughts that have been mentioned in this volume. Roger Brown (1988) brought our attention to the centrality of group deliberations in moving our judgments up the moral ladder: in trying to make a moral decision as a group, we must come to terms with others' points of view, which we usually need not do when we are making moral decisions by ourselves. This idea is central to our story and leads me to comment on the importance of the word "cooperation," not only to Larry but also to Piaget in the work from which Larry began. The idea of cooperation was important to Piaget, both within and beyond his work on moral development. He pointed out that the word "cooperation" consists of "co-operation"—carrying out operations together. Cooperation is one of the major factors in decentering, in moving beyond any given egocentric tendency. As Brown said, when we have to express to someone else our reasons for thinking as we do, our ideas become clearer for ourselves. Cooperation both is made possible by and gives rise to operations. In the same vein I refer to Edelstein's (this volume) remark that philosophers should not forget that all of us start with action, a point that Scheffler (this volume) has also made. Yet, the idea that universals take on their meaning through particulars is most central here (see Blum, this volume). That idea leads me to present my contribution in the form of a story.

This chapter presents a story for Larry Kohlberg. It takes place in Joanne Cleary's third-grade classroom in Cambridge, Massachusetts. Joanne was one of the committee members who helped organize the sessions on disarmament and peace. She was part of a group that had spent a long, difficult time trying to clarify their own feelings and thoughts about the issues that they talked about with children. The story presented here took place some years after the initial efforts of thinking about useful ways to work with children on issues of peace and justice.

A Story of Conflict

The children had gone down with the student teacher to the music room, and I stayed in the classroom. About ten or fifteen minutes later, Jeremy came back by himself, very upset, quivering, his shirt torn, and nearly unable to speak. After some prodding, he told me his story: The music teacher was absent, and the substitute had not yet come. The children were with Martha, the student teacher, sitting and waiting for the substitute. "Arthur was fighting with me because I sat in his chair. I didn't know it was his chair. It was empty and I sat in it. Arthur came and yelled at me and grabbed me and then ripped my shirt. Everyone was yelling at me." Jeremy clearly led me to believe that he was the victim. "Everyone was against me. It's been like this all year. I don't really have any friends here."

My bleeding heart sympathized with Jeremy's story. I was convinced that he had been bullied out of his seat. I suggested that we needed to talk about this incident with the group and I asked if he wanted to be there during the discussion. He said no, not really, so I let him go off to tutoring class. He was very upset emotionally, and I did not want him to be the center of attention in that condition. At that point I did not know that he was part of the problem.

Shortly thereafter, the others returned from a disappointing class that the substitute never attended. Immediately, I questioned Martha about the fight. She was sure that Jeremy was definitely not an innocent victim. That was when the circumstances of the fight started to become clearer to me and I knew this was going to be a teaching situation. Conflict resolution was part of a particular theme I had been focusing on with this group because there were a lot of little squabbles between the children and they were not able to understand their roles in the squabbles. The classroom gathering was a great opportunity because everybody was present and everybody had seen the fight between Jeremy and Arthur.

Jeremy was retrieved from tutoring. I told him he needed to be in the classroom discussion since I thought that he was avoiding his involvement in the instigation of this fight. First, I wanted to have everybody tell what they had seen and heard. I had them sit in a "community circle" and I tried to screen opinions and corroborate the different versions of the sequence of events—not an easy task! Arthur told his view, Jeremy told his view, and most of the others told their views. They all had been in one fight or another, and they all had their allegiances to either Arthur or Jeremy. So they all had something to say.

It was established that the auditorium was in total darkness when everyone arrived. The substitute was expected any moment. Martha was leading the group in the customary way of beginning music class: Those that could play the piano would take turns playing a piece and the others would watch and listen. Arthur got up to play his piece and Jeremy, who had been sitting in the second row, jumped, climbed, or otherwise moved into Arthur's seat in the front row. Arthur returned to his seat and Jeremy was in it. Arthur asked Jeremy to "please" move. Jeremy refused. Arthur was more forceful: "Move!" Still, Jeremy refused. Arthur grabbed Jeremy and ripped his shirt, and then somehow the two ended up on the floor. The others watched, some shouted "Go, Jer," others "Go, Arthur." At this point Martha intervened and gave both the opportunity to come back to the classroom to resolve this conflict with me. Arthur had the seat by then, so only Jeremy came back.

I decided that we had to determine how Jeremy had jumped. If he really had jumped, then did that mean he knew he was doing something wrong and had to do it fast so no one would see him until he got there? Or was the seat really vacant for a long time, and did he look around and see that nobody really cared? I got up and demonstrated the alternatives while they all watched. And then I had Jeremy get up and show me how he did it. And all the kids shouted, "No you didn't!" This was hard for Jeremy because he had to acknowledge what he had done.

Then, when Arthur returned to his seat and asked Jeremy to "please move," Jeremy refused, shook his head, and folded his arms across his chest. We had a lot of discussion at that point about different ways of folding your arms across your chest, and shaking your head, and again we demonstrated alternatives. We decided that Jeremy's was very much an aggressive folding of the arms, a tightening up, meaning "No, I'm not moving."

As far as Arthur was concerned, we talked about how he had said "please." We decided that he had not said a sweet, "Would you please move?" Arthur kept saying, "I asked him more than once," and I got the impression that, in his fashion, that was probably true. He also said he felt badly about tearing the shirt, but I reminded him that he had also said, "If you don't move I'm gonna rip your shirt again."

And then we discussed the why's. Why did Arthur want the seat so much that he was willing to fight about it? Why did Jeremy want the seat so much? At that point only Jeremy and Arthur spoke. Nobody else was permitted to say anything. Jeremy said that he had always wanted a front row seat. He usually didn't get one. Arthur kept getting up and Jeremy saw that empty seat, and he decided to take it. In fact, he had been hoping just before the music class that he would get a front row seat.

Arthur wanted to have that seat because it was next to Sam. Usually, when he and Sam sat together, they would poke and kick and tease each other. They were always getting separated. But that day they had been getting along fine. Arthur wanted to get back to the seat in order to continue his new, low-key interaction with Sam.

I asked, then, if each understood the other's point of view. Both said, with genuine surprise, "I didn't know that [about the other]." To me that was the whole lesson. That was the point where I said to myself, "It's been worth it." This was really what the whole discussion had been for.

But the teaching session was not yet complete. Next, I asked the rest of the class how they had contributed to the fight. We discussed taking sides, cheering, saying nothing out loud, but saying a lot with your body. We discussed getting help, walking away, doing nothing. We discussed what they could have done: separate the two fighters, explain to Jeremy that Arthur was in the seat a minute ago, call Martha right away. Then we discussed what Arthur could have done: seek Martha's help, continue to reason with Jeremy. And we discussed what Jeremy could have done: explain to someone the reason he wanted the seat and see if they would change with him, try to be first in line going to music class in order to get the seat he wanted.

Even with all of this discussion, I kept getting the sense that, for many of the children, and certainly for Jeremy, Arthur was the bully and Jeremy was the injured one. For Jeremy, in particular, it was still hard to see that his jumping into the seat from the row behind was an aggressive act and contributed to the conflict, as did his sitting with his arms folded across his chest—that silence was not so "golden" in this case. This sense was confirmed when I finally asked, "What can we do to resolve the conflict?"

Someone dutifully responded, "I think they should shake hands and say they are sorry." Arthur was willing, but not Jeremy. He said, "I can't do that right now." I respected Jeremy's feelings about that. So I explained that shaking hands did not necessarily mean that he was admitting sole guilt, that I was not suggesting that the fight was all his fault. Rather, I was saying that he was definitely responsible in part for it, and that he needed to acknowledge his responsibility. Shaking hands would be an acknowledgment of his regret that the fight happened and that he had some understanding of the other person's point of view.

I suggested that the two shake hands later. "Between now and the end of the day I want you to find a time when you're comfortable enough to say you're sorry, or to shake hands." The next day I approached Jeremy and he said that they had played together at recess and everything was okay now. He was finally able to accept that he had not simply been an innocent victim in the fight.

Thereafter during the school year, every time we wanted to talk about understanding someone else's point of view, we referred back to this fight. It was a good lesson on cooperation and conflict resolution.

The Essence of Moral Education

This story illustrates what Larry wrote about years earlier when moral education curriculum consisted of having the children discuss the research dilemmas that he described. He called this a "one-way street model," and he argued that a psychologist should not simply take a theory, developed and tested by pure developmental psychological research, start to apply the theory and make prescriptions from the theory to classroom practice, and then evaluate the effect by that theory rather than formative research. Rather, he believed that you had to be in reciprocal collaboration with teachers. He said that the one-way street model of relating theory to practice "rests on what I have called 'the psychologist's fallacy,' " that is, the belief that what is important for developmental psychology research is the same as what is important for practitioners in the classroom. That view is similar to the subject discussed in Duckworth (1987). It is as if the goal of moral education is to get the right answer to Larry's dilemmas, and the goal of science or mathematics education is to go through the experiments that Piaget happened to devise as a psychologist. The story presented here illustrates the importance of helping children think about moral issues in their lives as they live them.

For some time I have thought that Piaget's central message for education is that intelligence develops by being used. It occurs to me that moral judgment, and perhaps even moral action, do likewise.

References

Brown, R. Remarks addressed to "The Legacy of Lawrence Kohlberg" symposium, Graduate School of Education, Harvard University, April 15, 1988.

Duckworth, E. " 'Either We're Too Early and They Can't Get It, or We're Too Late and They Know It Already': The Dilemma of Applying Piaget." In *"The Having of Wonderful Ideas" and Other Essays on Teaching and Learning.* New York: Teachers College Press, 1987.

Eleanor Duckworth is professor of Education, Graduate School of Education, Harvard University. She is author of the book The Having of Wonderful Ideas *(1987).*

Joanne Cleary is a teacher at Tobin Elementary School in Cambridge, Massachusetts.

The just community approach to moral education is applied to a prison setting.

The Prison as a Just Community

Kelsey Kauffman

Lawrence Kohlberg surprised many people with his conceptions of the child as a moral philosopher. He confounded the popular wisdom even more by regarding inmates and prison officers as moral philosophers. What a setting in which to be a moral philosopher! Of all public institutions in our society, prisons operate at perhaps the lowest moral level: they are the least democratic, the least just, the least likely to be perceived as fair by their inhabitants.

Although my own research on Massachusetts' prison officers was not directly concerned with Kohlberg's theories of moral development, it focused on many of the moral issues central to prison life. The sixty officers who were part of my study characterized the problems they faced on a daily basis as moral problems, ones involving discrepancies between their own moral values and the behavior expected of them as officers. These were men working in maximum-security prisons where officers and inmates were locked in violent, at times deadly, struggle. Yet many officers went to great lengths to refrain from harming inmates. For example, in an interview with an experienced officer who was highly regarded by his fellow officers, I asked if he would shoot an escaping inmate. He responded as follows:

> I think it's like a lot of things that they say, "This is your job and it's right." I can't see it as being right. I can't accept it. I can't. I couldn't live with it.... Inside of me there's two parts. One that says I read the post orders and I [am] standing here with my loaded gun and I know what to do. But then there's always that other guy that's inside and it says, "If you do it, what happens to *you* afterwards?" I mean, you can

take my uniform and hang it up in the hall of fame for correction officers and say I hit the guy three times in the head. But it's an empty uniform. The person that was in there is gone, is destroyed and is no longer. Some guys can live with it and say, "Yup, that's my uniform." But I couldn't. I just couldn't accept that.

This officer was "scared of permanently hurting" an inmate not only because of what that would mean for the inmate but also because he believed that in the process he would destroy what he valued about himself. Like most other officers, he had no doubts about the nature of the moral dilemmas he faced. Regardless of whether officers became active participants in the worst abuses of their prisons or were merely passive observers, the moral compromises involved exact a terrible toll.

Kohlberg understood the moral debilitation inherent in prison life and prison work. He, Joseph Hickey, and Peter Scharf set out in the early 1970s to demonstrate that it was possible to establish a "just community" within a traditional prison. That is, they wanted to create a prison democracy within a prison autocracy. Clearly, Kohlberg was an optimist and had great faith in his own theories.

At the Connecticut State Prison for Women, Kohlberg and his associates established a just community in a self-contained unit that housed twenty-five inmates and six members of the prison staff. The unit operated according to rules and procedures accepted as fair by inmates and staff. Together they wrote their own constitution, devised their own rules, and, with some limitations, maintained their own discipline and applied their own punishments.

The unit's governance was handled in community meetings that could be called at any time. Inmates and officers had one vote each. Issues were discussed and were occasionally decided by majority vote. More often, meetings stayed in session until a consensus emerged, even if that required six, eight, or even ten hours. In addition to the community meetings, inmates and staff convened in smaller groups once or twice a week to discuss more personal concerns. Staff were trained to guide discussions, whether in community meetings or small groups, toward a moral dialogue. The goal was to focus the group's attention on moral aspects of problems confronting the unit and its members.

The unit operated for about eight years. Was it a success? The prison's administrators were usually satisfied. If nothing else, many so-called problem inmates made their peace in the democratic unit. As an officer who had previously worked in traditional parts of the prison, I thought it was a great success. I did not know or particularly care about moral development theory, but I did like the structure of the democratic unit because it offered a way out of the endless conflicts and deceptions of prison life.

In certain respects the staff in the democratic unit were less powerful than staff in the rest of the prison. After all, in the democratic unit, staff could easily be outvoted on any issue. But in other respects they were much more powerful. Most important, the program provided officers a legitimacy for their authority that officers in other parts of the prison lacked. It also helped compensate for handicaps most officers face when competing with inmate "heavies" for power within a prison. After all, inmates substantially outnumber officers and usually have greater knowledge about what is happening within the prison world. In addition, the threat that inmate "heavies" pose to recalcitrant inmates is usually far more potent than the threat officers pose. Inmates usually have more to fear from each other than from officers, which is why prison officials who attempt to establish their regimes on the basis of coercion often fare so badly.

Most inmates and officers perceived the democratic unit as just and fair. In that sense alone, it was a triumph. Most participants also came to perceive the unit as supportive and caring. It was a situation in which it was difficult not to learn a great deal about others and oneself, and about the moral nexus between the two.

Data suggest that a number of inmates in the program moved to higher moral stages in their reasoning (Hickey and Scharf, 1980, chap. 6). Whether the unit served more traditional rehabilitation goals is another matter. The program undoubtedly helped some inmates avoid future imprisonment. For a good many others, it did not. Kohlberg never sought to justify the unit on such traditional grounds; that it served the ends of social justice was sufficient (Hickey and Scharf, 1980; Kohlberg, Kauffman, Scharf, and Hickey, 1974).

What can we learn from this experiment?

If tomorrow I became superintendent of a prison similar to the one where Kohlberg established his democratic unit, I would attempt to run at least a portion of the prison along lines developed by Kohlberg and his colleagues. That is, I would attempt to have inmates and staff work together to establish and live by rules and procedures that were perceived as just and fair by both groups. I would do so not merely because of my own convictions regarding what constitutes a "just" institution but also because obtaining the consent of those to be governed—even if they are felons—is an effective way to govern over the long haul.

Having said that, I must tell you that I do not think the experiment and its results are particularly relevant to conditions in most American prisons today. The prison within which the democratic unit operated was small, had a mostly nonviolent inmate population, and contained discrete living units. It also had a supportive prison superintendent and state commissioner of correction. Those are elements not easily found in American prisons today, most of which have cavernous cell blocks, entrenched patterns of inmate-on-inmate violence, embattled staff, severe overcrowding, and shortages of officers.

Kohlberg's just community within the confines of a traditional prison was a worthy experiment. It serves as a model of what could be. However, I believe that Kohlberg's greatest legacy in regard to prisons is in making us aware of the moral consequences of operating prison systems according to moral and legal principles that are markedly inferior to those that apply to the larger community. The presence of enclaves of brutality and deprivation, created and sustained by governments on behalf of citizens, literally demoralizes—that is, corrupts the morals of—the society as a whole. As Kohlberg would have reminded us, contradictions inherent in maintaining such morally "inferior" institutions are as apparent for the society that creates them as they are for the individuals who work and live within them. Inevitably, the moral standards of the greater community are undermined.

References

Hickey, J., and Scharf, P. *Toward a Just Correctional System: Experiments in Implementing Democracy in Prisons.* San Francisco: Jossey-Bass, 1980.

Kohlberg, L., Kauffman, K., Scharf, P., and Hickey, J. *The Just Community Approach to Corrections: A Manual.* Cambridge, Mass.: Moral Education Research Foundation, Graduate School of Education, Harvard University, 1974.

Kelsey Kauffman is author of Prison Officers and Their World *(1988) and continues to write about prisons.*

Moral discourse is used to create positive behavioral successes as well as long-term structural development.

Kohlberg's Educational Legacy

Fritz K. Oser

In the time before Lawrence Kohlberg visited Düsseldorf (Northrine-Westfalia) in 1985, there was a heated political discussion with regard to his theory. People from the right wing assumed it to be a new form of value relativism; leftists suspected it to be a new form of transmission of bourgeois values into children's minds. Then, when Kohlberg gave his lecture, both camps became very quiet and thoughtful. He was avoiding the devil of relativism as well as the deep blue sea of indoctrination. It was a new core idea that came up: a developmental approach embedded into a social participatory fabric of our everyday life, that is, the everyday life of our schools and of the instructional and learning processes.

Let me present you with an anecdote: Early one morning I came to a college (gymnasium) where a group of students and teachers were trying to build up a different kind of just community model. As I entered the school, a group of tenth-grade students confronted me in the hallway. They were angry. When I asked them to explain what was disturbing them, they told me about their perceptions of the "spring camp planning" lesson in which we all had participated the week before. Their first objection was that we had used them like guinea pigs in an experiment; second, their impression had been that we were lying to them, because we pretended that we were going to prepare a spring camp whereas, actually, we just discussed moral dilemmas with them; their third point was that we classified them by ascribing stages to their reasoning, which they experienced as a severe discrimination.

Now, what in fact had happened the previous week? I had been invited, together with some of my colleagues and a group of teachers, to attend a class given by a philosophy instructor in the school. During this class, he announced to the students and to us that he wanted to discuss and prepare a plan for a camp. Rather than doing that, he only introduced a hypothetical camp dilemma. Of course, the students felt misled and now they were expressing their anger and frustration to me. As you can see, an artificial hypothetical dilemma suddenly turned into a real-life conflict generated by a hidden curriculum where the students felt "used" by the instructor.

Later on, the teachers discussed the students' accusation. They recognized that they had to apologize to the students and really begin talking to them about their concerns, about new programs, about democratic procedures, and so on. Out of the discussion that followed, the beginnings of a just, true, democratic community emerged. From this point on the school reform project really was in line with what Lawrence Kohlberg's educational work was and is all about.

The Genesis of a Just Community

Following the line of Kohlberg's work, I present here some information about the construction and the genesis of several just communities in various types of schools. I focus on what I think it means to adapt the Kohlbergian just community approach to a school system such as the German system. These school reform projects require (1) a set of fundamentally new educational considerations, which move away from knowledge acquisition to value reconstruction, and (2) a research program, which has to provide continuous assistance and care for the teachers involved. Both requirements are connected with difficult decision-making procedures concerning the understanding and practical realization of Kohlberg's core ideas.

The Relationship Between Kohlberg's Later and Earlier Work

Starting at a scientific level we have to attend to the fact that Kohlberg's work is not yet familiar to teachers as practitioners: Most people have access to the 1969 through 1974 work, but they have not yet completely grasped the idea of a comprehensive democratic education. Whoever wants to know Kohlberg's contribution in total has to start with his later theoretical accounts and practical models. In the time prior to his death these have shown an integrative force and have shed new light on all preceding parts of his work.

In their 1972 article, Kohlberg and Mayer postulated a certain way for instructional techniques to meet the challenge of stimulating development toward the higher stages. Several years later, this claim is embedded in the just community approach, that is, in a process of democratic schooling that involves collective establishment of rules and responsibility taking in concrete situations instead of hypothetical dilemma discussions. Thus, the old claim remains the same but is integrated into a new context. Conceptual changes initiate changes, or even turns, in the domain of research. In the case at hand, it is no longer enough to introduce and assess techniques of developmental intervention. We must also establish the conditions needed for such development in the real-life context of schools. This focus on concrete situations provides a means of coping with the problems of what has been called "the psychologist's fallacy." Moreover, there are also clearer outlines of the possibilities of developmental transition, a better equilibrium to the relationship between moral judgment and moral action, and a better differentiation and integration of rules. That is why I think that, in terms of educational viewpoints, the efforts to understand Kohlberg's theory should proceed "top-down," that is, from the later work to the earlier, which may also be considered "bottom-up," from the practice to the theory.

Moral Problems? We'll Fix 'Em!

On the practical level of schooling, we have to deal with the fact that German and Swiss schools have a consistent curricula countrywide; they are highly organized and overly controlled by the state. Thus, Kohlberg's approach to moral education evoked considerable discussion in Germany about the feasibility of school reform. For instance, legal matters were addressed, and the relevance of this kind of school democratization was questioned. The advisory board for the implementation of Kohlberg's ideas in different types of schools discussed these issues and formulated various plans over the course of a year and a half. There was no agreement on school reform until the results of implementations influenced some decisions for the board. After the first few weeks of practical work, several doubts had decisively diminished: it was not too difficult to involve parents, and it was not difficult at all to involve students and teachers in the program. Additionally, practice demonstrated that a narrowly defined "organizational creed" was unneeded; the just community idea could be adapted to different settings. The decision about whether to establish just communities in a limited number of grades or instead to pursue global restructuring of schools is a matter of adequacy and given political ranges; it should not be a matter of doctrines.

The main danger is unwillingness to see the positive challenge in "difficulties." Principals and teachers of many schools told us over and over again, "There are no *real* social or moral problems in our schools—we fix 'em." This is a way of undermining every substantial educational intervention. In actuality, there are more than enough conflicts calling for settlement in all of the schools. The turning point in the schools we work with is the understanding that moral problems not only have to be settled but also are material for learning purposes.

A Discourse-Oriented Attitude

A number of colleagues perceived the cognitive developmental approach as a means of solving behavior and discipline problems. Once I visited the "Haupt-school" in Langenfeld, which uses the just community model. The teachers welcomed me with a question: Does Kohlberg mean thumbs-up or thumbs-down? Thumbs-up meant laissez-faire, a permissive stance, whereas thumbs-down meant prevailing over problem behavior. It took a long series of discussions and exercises to make clear that the just community approach appeals to children's rationality. This stance, which presupposes that children are capable of being reasonable and responsible, we call a discourse-oriented attitude.

The effects of this approach in practice are astonishing. You can watch teachers realizing that fifth-graders are able to chair a community meeting with ninety students and twenty teachers participating; you observe teachers noticing that eleven-year-olds are able to convince ninth-graders that smoking in the restrooms is unfair to the community. This approach became effective immediately when the agenda committee proposed to discuss certain problems that students had with their teachers. This issue was handled in a very sensitive and responsible way. Another, more indirect effect of the "new style" was exemplified in the same school. After one Monday meeting, the agenda committee, consisting of three teachers and nine students, announced that teachers' frequent lateness for class (especially after the breaks) should be a subject for the next community meeting, which was to be on Friday. The topic was cancelled on Friday; no teacher was late for class during that week.

Long-Term Interventions Versus Quick Effects

Currently, four schools in Northrine-Westfalia utilize the just community approach, each of them in a particular way: a gymnasium, a "comprehensive school" (*Gesamtschule*), a "Haupt"-school and a "Real"-school (science oriented). With respect to all of these schools the most important aspect of the researchers' contribution is teacher education. The teachers need assistance every single week. Teachers are used to short-term interventions; once they decide to implement something new they expect immediate effects.

Long-term interventions are problematic because they require an understanding of slow structural transformation. Teachers ask, "How can these values ever emerge when we don't teach them directly?" It is hard to understand that the framework of values only refers to the higher moral principles and that everything else results from the students' work, their reconstruction of value systems. But, in general, the teachers in the just community schools are interested in matters of developmental psychology, of learning activities, of the formation of values, of the transformation of structures; they are even interested in the procedure of moral judgment scoring. And I believe that it is the just community practice itself that is motivating them.

Interrelated Pedagogical Principles Underlying the Just Community Approach

In order to introduce the just community into the traditional school structure, we try to make moral education accessible to the teachers by starting not only from insights of moral psychology but also from traditional principles of the facilitation of learning. Examples of these principles are (1) learning by acting, by doing, by confrontation with the object and by personal experience (active reconstruction of reality); (2) identification by participation (generation of norms); (3) development of responsibility by being able to be responsible; (4) role taking or empathy opportunities; (5) a positive pedagogical presupposition: the child is always able to participate fully, to care, to decide, and so on; (6) mutual commitment of teachers and students (which includes an element of love); and (7) development as the aim of education.

These principles are interrelated. They are maxims of action; they are to be validated in real-life spheres. Teachers must learn to direct their courses of action on the basis of these principles and, by this means, to achieve confidence in the quality of their work.

Professional Morality: The Teacher's Ethos

Each teaching act implies hidden moral aspects. In choosing an instructional method, for example, the teacher has to be concerned about the "just" (equal) possibility of each child to learn. Each child must have the same optimal arrangement. How is this possible?

Professional morality cannot be understood simply by assessing moral judgment stages. Rather, in each professional decision the teacher has to balance claims of justice, care, and truthfulness. And this balance can have different procedural features. Procedural features refer to what has empirically turned out to be a relatively clear conception of professional methods. We distinguish five types of such procedural balances (see Oser, Patry, Zutavern, and Hafliger, 1987):

1. *Avoiding.* The teacher tries to solve a problem by not facing it. In these cases, someone else will have to maintain the balance.

2. *Delegating.* The teacher basically accepts that he or she has some

responsibility for dealing with a problem, but in order to maintain a sense of security, he or she tries to adjourn the decision making and either to share the burden with or to shift the responsibility to some authority (for example, the principal or a psychologist).

3. *Single-handed decision making.* The teacher tries to settle the problem *ex auctoritate,* by taking it solely into his or her hands. Decision making does not involve the interested parties but is followed through by the teacher (as "expert"), quickly and oftentimes in an authoritarian manner.

4. *Discourse I.* The teacher accepts his or her personal responsibility for settling a problem and subscribes to the task of balancing justice, care, and truthfulness in each new situation. The viewpoints taken are justified, and the teacher is committed to a good life (as a legitimate interest on behalf of the students) and a just environment. However, the whole burden rests on the teacher's own shoulders.

5. *Discourse II.* The teacher acts in the Discourse I orientation but, in addition, presupposes that each student (and any other person who is concerned and involved) is, in a deep sense, a rational human being who is also interested in and capable of balancing justice, care, and truthfulness. This holds even in critical or aggressive situations.

Teacher education should help teachers become Discourse II educators. I believe that only Discourse II-type persons are pedagogically giving their best. Eventually, only they are able to create a just community and to participate fully in it. This is why intervention studies are done: to transform Discourse I decisions into Discourse II decisions, and thus to learn more about the dynamics of a just interaction.

One of the major differences between American and European versions of the just community approach is that the former are concerned more with the participatory structure itself, the latter with the fundamental attitudes of the teachers, their subjective theories about democracy, and their problems concerning processes of community building. One of our new ways of examining these interventions is to look at the relationship between Discourse II procedures and Kohlberg's stages.

Kohlberg: Remember His Pedagogical Work

In closing, let me return to Lawrence Kohlberg. In my view, the development of his just communities is one of the most important fundamentals for school reform in the 1980s. In terms of biography, it is the crowning event of his work. In designing and validating his developmental theory, Kohlberg's genius was steadily ahead of his capacity to realize his ideas; all the time the differentiation was stronger and more pronounced than the integration and stabilization of the new. In contrast, his work in the schools developed in a step-by-step manner, integrating the affective and cognitive as well as the conative/actional features of moral learning and, furthermore, requiring commitment to the child and social engagement in schools.

Maybe Kohlberg broke under his own commitment. Maybe he saw that true school reform cannot be institutionalized and that it stands and falls with the reformer's and the teacher's commitment. There are a lot of educationalists with big ideas. There are only a very few who have great ideas *and* try to put them into practice. Kohlberg was one of the few. It is because of his course of pedagogical action that he will be remembered in one and the same breath with educational giants like Johann Heinrich Pestalozzi, Maria Montessori, Janusz Korczak, and Paulo Freire.

References

Kohlberg, L., and Mayer, R. "Development as the Aim of Education." *Harvard Educational Review*, 1972, *42*, 449-496.

Oster, Patry, Zutavern, and Haflinger. "Professional Ethos of Teachers: Why Do Teachers Solve Problems in Different Ways?" In *Forschungen zur Professionsmoral. Lehrerethos als positive Einstellung.* Verpflichtung und Gerechtigkeit. Report no. 3, Freiburg: Pädagogisches Institut/Universität Freiburg, 1987.

Fritz K. Oser is professor of education, University of Fribourg. He continues to implement Kohlberg's just community approach to moral education in German and Swiss schools.

Kohlberg inspires confidence and encourages teachers to develop moral programs in schools.

Some Personal Reflections on Larry Kohlberg as Teacher of Teachers

Edwin Fenton

In this chapter, as in my address at the symposium, I want to be anecdotal, a privilege generally accorded to graying people in their late sixties.

My anecdotes date back as far as 1972, for me a very difficult year, which I spent as a visiting scholar on the third floor of Harvard's Larsen Hall—the Moral Mecca of the world. The year presented difficulties because I was killing my intellectual offspring. For a decade, I had been developing social studies programs for secondary-school students. My colleagues and I had written materials for eight courses, each with a new style textbook, an audio-visual kit, a teachers' guide, and a testing program, but even before I arrived, I had begun to recognize some of the shortcomings of these materials. Larry and his colleagues increased my uneasiness as they helped me to learn new ways to think about social studies education. Often, I told Larry about the trials and tribulations of typical teachers in typical schools. I did not, of course, define typical. During this mutual exchange, Larry and I became both colleagues and friends. We had joint grants and joint publications to cement our collegial relationship, and fishing and oystering expeditions in Wellfleet Harbor to foster our friendship.

We initially had met two years before at the Stone Foundation. I always thought that the Stone grant to Larry and the Carnegie-Mellon group was conscience money because Mr. Stone had given Nixon so many millions. He gave us far less money. We had been working for two years to develop what I liked to call "civic dilemmas" and Larry called "moral dilemmas." (You see, I had to face school boards where the word "moral" got me into immediate trouble. Make what you will of that comment about American education.) Larry was conducting research on cognitive moral development. He and I worked with a number of people both locally and across the country to help teachers learn how to lead dilemma discussions, write dilemmas, and carry on research.

Then the Danforth Foundation blessed us with an additional grant. Perhaps that was more conscience money because Danforth gave so much money to Washington University instead of to Harvard or Carnegie-Mellon. I took the first year of that grant period to come to Harvard in order to develop a more theoretical justification for what I had been doing for the previous ten years. I had already published eight social studies books, and, pretty much dissatisfied with the work we had done, I was thinking about a second edition. I was living on the third floor of Dick Graham's house and came into Larsen Hall daily to work and talk to colleagues. Every night I returned home and sat down at my typewriter. I wrote short papers to myself because that is how I have always learned best, by writing out my ideas. I wrote a number of short papers, which I still have in my files.

I began my series of papers by contending that projects should not respond primarily to a single performance gap the way educators did after Sputnik. Next, I argued that no one should be given money to run a curriculum project unless they first went into a school and taught a full schedule for a semester from the books that were there—that is, taught typical courses to typical students in typical schools—as a way of finding out first hand what the territory is like. Again, I did not define typical. This principle derived partly from Larry's behavior. He spent much of his time for several years working in the Cluster School at Cambridge Rindge and Latin. I was very proud of that paper about the necessity of teaching experience. I also wrote a long paper to myself about the necessity for a developmental approach to social studies education, instead of assuming that all eighth-graders were formal operational, Stage 5 thinkers.

After a few weeks in my capacity as visiting scholar, Larry said to me, "Ted, what are you writing?" and I said, "I'm writing a stack of papers." And he said, "Want me to look at them?" and I said, "Sure." I brought the stack in the next day and Larry started to skim. For those who never saw Larry skim, I can attest that it was an amazing sight: glance down a page, turn it, glance again, turn again, scratch his wrist, turn again, and so on in bewildering rapidity. In ten minutes, he had examined my weeks of steady labor. Then he said, "Ted, I think you're doing all right." He didn't say that in a deprecating way. I took him to mean "What you are saying is really very sensible."

We had a long talk about it. Then he made a typical, humane Larry comment. He said something like, "I think that you're too tough on yourself and what you have done. You're looking at the issue too narrowly." Larry was always able to look at the essence of an issue and then step back and see what surrounded it. He said, "You say that you are dissatisfied with a lot of the materials you have published. Maybe they will go out of use, and therefore the project that you have been working on hasn't been a success. But think about what you and I and our colleagues have been doing for the past couple of years and think about what has been happening to the teachers who have worked with us. Think of all the new stuff they have read." Perhaps Larry didn't say "stuff." That wasn't part of his vocabulary. "Remember how they went to class excited with new materials, new ideas, and new ways of working in the schools. Look at how they learned to work with each other, work as members of a team, as members of a community. Remember how they learned with students in new and meaningful ways. Think about their new image of students. Instead of viewing that tenth-grade student who has cheated as a rotten kid, they have learned to see him as a developing human being, thinking appropriately and acting in the same way, growing into a human being who can be thinking about societal maintenance and, eventually, justice, if we give him the opportunity to do so in school." I think the kind of teachers Larry effected made schools much better places, and that is a part of the rich heritage he left to us.

Larry also talked to me about the effects of experimental school programs on students—the same issue from the other side of the desk. No, that's not right. Larry would never have separated students from teachers with desks. "You start to see students excited about real issues," he pointed out. Larry and I had tested a dozen or so versions of what we called "Sharon's dilemma," a story in which Sharon must deal with her friend Jill's act of thievery. We drafted version after version and tried them out with student after student in classes all over this country and parts of Europe. The dilemma raises a vital issue to students: Do you tell on your friends or do you abide by the law? Students were enormously excited about that issue. "Look at the way students discussing Sharon's dilemma participated in classes," he said, "the shy kid at the rear of the room who never said anything was suddenly excited about Sharon and Jill. Look at the slow but steady growth that went on."

Recently, one of these students, now my colleague at Carnegie-Mellon, turned up in my office. He said, "Ted, I just turned in a grant proposal to the National Science Foundation to develop new science material for elementary school students." I said to him, as is my duty as a senior member of the faculty, "What does that mean for your tenure decision?" He said, "Oh my God, Ted, not you too; that's what everyone in the department asks. Frankly, I don't give a damn. I learned so much from the teachers I had in elementary and secondary schools that I think, even putting tenure at risk, that I want to repay them in kind."

Larry had dozens of students who echo this attitude. They cared about students in their classes, they were determined to make the society a better place, and they threw themselves into this vital work. Most of them who taught in universities also earned tenure. Larry had set for them an excellent example of how to combine superb scholarship and excellent teaching with service to the community in schools, temples, churches, prisons, universities, and dozens of other institutions. We may never see his brand of excellence again.

Edwin Fenton is professor of history and director of the University Teaching Center at Carnegie-Mellon University. He is involved in teacher training and the implementation of moral education in social studies curricula.

*Paradoxes between the substance and procedure of
moral education are examined from a societal perspective.*

Lawrence Kohlberg's Socratic Paradox

Wolfgang Edelstein

Will Socrates make the world a better place? The question, I think, discloses a basic paradox in Lawrence Kohlberg's work. The paradox is that of simultaneously seeking the truth and doing the good, an offshoot of the naturalistic fallacy that claims the unity of epistemology and morality, of is and ought. Space limitations here preclude a full unraveling of the intricacies of this paradox in Kohlberg's work, so I instead provide a few glimpses of its practical importance.

The Analogy Between Lawrence Kohlberg and Socrates

There is no question that Kohlberg identifies Socrates as an exemplar of the highest, principled stage of moral maturity. The exemplariness of Socrates refers to the *substance* of his judgments and the *method* used to reach them. The substance represents recognition of the ultimate state of rightness and goodness. The method is the unrelenting and critical questioning of prevailing beliefs. In the *Apology*, Plato has Socrates describe how he goes about fostering virtue to the detriment of the bag-of-virtues approach that Everyman cherishes. Virtue is a universal, logically consistent concept of moral adequacy that determines action and provides a standard for the community at large. This concept is pitted against the particular notions of the common good and individual duty as held by unenlightened individuals. Progress is initiated in cognitive action upon individuals—by questioning them and by involving them in contradictions, or rather by disclosing to them, through the dynamics of truth-revealing dialogues, the contradictions in which their unreflected positions keep them trapped. This is the gadfly activity, legitimated by the Delphian God. As a gadfly, Socrates is subjecting citizens to the Piagetian clinical method, probing for truth and understanding, and they are expected to grow. I take it for granted that Kohlberg identified with Socrates.

I believe that the analogy between Socrates and Kohlberg is neither fortuitous nor unconscious. The structural similarity between Kohlberg's moral dilemmas and those reported in the Platonic dialogues is not a surface affair. The methodological analogies have already been roughly delineated. The educational intent is an additional indicator. In the *Apology*, Socrates makes it clear that his goal is the virtue of the City, achieved through the transformation of individuals. The accusation against Socrates—that he corrupted young people—implies this socio-educational intent. The tragic aspect of moral perfection is a point Kohlberg dwells on by implication, by choosing his moral heroes among the tragic figures. Tragedy is stressed by the nonutilitarian structure of his dilemmas, which, in truth, have no logical solutions but rather only individual resolutions. And Socrates' self-characterization of his role, the function of the gadfly, oddly reminds us of Kohlberg's provocatively insouciant response to the conventions and expectations of his peers.

The Gadfly as Moral Provocateur

The activity of provoking moralization through the discovery of moral contradiction and disequilibration discloses an additional aspect of the basic paradox: moral development for the virtue of the City versus social structure against virtue. Can the City accommodate the activity of a gadfly? This is the question behind the *Apology*, and the tragedy of Socrates. For Plato, who was not a pragmatist, the answer is no—and thus no to democracy, indicted for its verdict against Socrates. For Kohlberg, who is a pragmatist thinker, the answer is an optimistic yes. For us, in hindsight, the issue appears unresolved, and if we consider the future, disturbing.

Let us translate the drama of Socrates into less poetic terms: How well adapted is the moralization message to the conditions of its social transmission? Can it be transferred from the context of individual disequilibration in discursive relationships based on the mutual assent of adults, and introduced into the context of the institutional order of the schools and the education system, that is, into the instructional activities of adults in relation to the captive audience of children and adolescents? Can it be transferred into the curricula, school structures, and principles of instruction?

In view of questions about the institutional conditions of education, let us ask again, can Socrates make the world a better place? Does the Socratic program provide us with a method, a principle for the design of educational environments? From the successes and failures of education in the service of development, have we learned the necessary lessons about conditions of success in the institutional order of mass education? Have we acquired the necessary knowledge about the reformability of the system and the probabilities of rejection?

Facing the paradox between substance and procedure, between the message of principled morality and the method of constructive disequilibration, only the option of procedure appears to be compatible with the nature of public education, with the institutional structure of mass education, and with the administrative patterns of state power. (And even this option may be in doubt, as I briefly discuss in a moment.) The meaning of this option for public education is that we may be forced to choose between the *substantive core* of Kohlberg's moral theory, that is, moral development and moralization, and his *methodological imperative*, that is, development as the aim of education. This choice, of course, has nothing to do with the validity of the moral theory, which undoubtedly is a major milestone in the development of a formal yet psychologically realistic theory of ethics. But since, in a fallible world, the theory is bound to be intrinsically imperfect, it by necessity arouses the ideological animosity of the separate but intermeshed camps of educational traditionalists, perfectionists, realists, and minimalists. Remember the grand jury in the case of "Athens against Socrates."

In addition to the ideological objections, there are other obstacles that stem from the secularist structure of public education, its plurality of purposes, and the compromise patterns of institutional value allegiances. There are technical objections that stem from the high level of instructional skills required in developmental education and the demands on teacher competence and teacher compassion. Cognitively and emotionally overburdened teachers can be formidable enemies of even the most admirable reforms.

A Case Study of Educational Intervention

Recently, Fritz Oser (1987) differentiated various forms of educational intervention that extend between what I call the substance-based versus procedure-based poles of moral education in the Kohlberg tradition. These orientations reach from the just community approach through special workshops and specific dilemma discussions within schools, to integration of moral education into the disciplinary context of school curricula. Commitment to the full thrust of substantive moral education increases as intervention moves toward the just community. Near this substantive pole, participation, in principle, is dependent on the assent of those involved, which, under liberal constitutional principles, is voluntary and private. Otherwise, it would be considered indoctrination and thus a contradiction in terms.

In order to maximize acceptability within the public order of education, we therefore turn to the other, methodological pole of Kohlberg's system. No doubt, to an informed mind, the notion of development as the aim of education—in its precise, technical, instructional, and curricular meaning—implies a liberating transformation of the educational experience. I cannot develop the proof for this contention here. Accept it as true for the moment, as I focus on the vicissitudes of an attempt to introduce this ideologically innocent but strongly transformative version of Kohlberg's educational heritage into the educational system of an entire country.

For the systemic reasons mentioned above, the reform strategy pursued in Iceland during the period 1974–1984 was based on what roughly amounts to the most procedurally oriented form of Oser's typology: integration into regular, if reformed, disciplinary contexts. Specifically, under official sanction, the disciplines of history, geography, civics, sociology, anthropology, and economics were transformed into a broadly based social studies curriculum, extending through the nine grades of the compulsory school program of Iceland (Edelstein, 1986). Encompassing opportunities for moral discussions wherever relevant to the learning task, the entire curriculum was based on cognitive developmental principles of induction, discussion and contradiction, comparison and contrast, and cognitive conflict and re-equilibration (Taba, 1962; Bruner, 1966). Kohlberg's imperative of development as the aim of education was thus the basis of operations.

Overall, these reforms were successful and became a cornerstone of the general syllabus and an accepted model of curriculum construction in most subject matter areas. The influence extended into teacher education and teacher in-service training, shaping the didactic and professional consciousness of teachers at both the primary- and secondary-school levels.

Even with due consideration to conformism, ignorance, sloth, and attrition in the day-to-day administration of the schools, the reforms did work. Kohlberg's inspiration led to a period of reform activism and enthusiasm that reached beyond individual leadership, individual schools, and individual teachers. For a while, theory indeed turned practical. It worked as a generative matrix for school reform for more than a decade. Those involved in fact believed that Kohlberg's theory of developmental education was helping to make the world, or at least Iceland's schools, a better place.

Progress is a many splendored thing, but it is very vulnerable. Only the advent of a government composed of a right-of-center majority was needed to stop the project, politically at least. The new Conservatives joined forces with the new intellectual Right to seize power over education (Edelstein, 1986). In Parliament and in the media, they vociferously voiced the new consensus: allegedly, the protagonists of developmental education were either unwittingly or intentionally destroying the schools and corrupting the young; this was a subversion of national values. A monograph by a philosophy professor and president of the Icelandic Psychological Association singled out Jean Piaget and Lawrence Kohlberg as the false prophets that had subverted education, through either the ignorance or intentional malevolence of the so-called educational experts. (Recall Adelson and Finn's 1985 attack on peace education in the United States, directed toward those who were insidiously called the "tenured left.") The grand jury was hatching its verdict. The general public looked on in silence, unmoved.

The Final Socratic Paradox

While Kohlberg's doctrine of developmental education had proved essentially successful, it aroused such political and intellectual rage that its progress was arrested by a decision of the Ministry of Education following a series of highly focused press attacks. The protectors of the polity turned against development as the aim of education, alleging corruption of the quality of the schools and the loyalty of the young. Is this outburst of hostility against the idea of development, cognitive and moral, related to the Socratic nature of the theory under attack? Does it speak for, or against, the strength of Kohlberg's theory to contribute to a better world, that it raises the wrath and the irony of both cultural relativists and institutionalists and unites both liberals and conservatives of many camps in opposition to his program? I do not know the answers to these questions. But they certainly raise a point about society's taken-for-granted use of education for power and for law and order.

It is interesting that both moral theory and developmental education come under attack. Whether Kohlberg's theory of moral education is generalizable across schools may be in doubt. His theory of developmental education, however, clearly has the force to transform the schools. But whether it will be allowed to prove the point of evolutionary rationality and turn the schools into better places will depend on who eventually is proved correct, Plato or Dewey. Unfortunately, today, Dewey's pragmatism is accorded little educational credit, and Socrates and Kohlberg are dead, leaving us not answers but instead a legacy of burning questions.

References

Adelson, J., and Finn, C. E., Jr. "Terrorizing Children." *Commentary*, 1985, *79*, 29-36.

Bruner, J. S. *Towards a Theory of Instruction.* Cambridge, Mass.: Harvard University Press, 1966.

Edelstein, W. "The Rise and Fall of the Social Science Curriculum Project in Iceland, 1974-1984: Reflections on Reasons and Power in Educational Progress." *Journal of Curriculum Studies*, 1986, *19*, 1-23.

Oser, F. "Moglichkeiten und Grenzen der Anwendun des Kohlbergschen Konzepts der moralischen Erziehung in unseren Schulen" [Prohibition and limits of the application of Kohlberg's concept of moral education in our schools]. In G. Lind and J. Raschert (eds.), *Moralische Urteilsfahigkeit. Eine Auseinandersetzung mit Lawrence Kohlberg.* Weinheim: Beltz, 1987.

Taba, H. *Curriculum Development: Theory and Practice.* San Diego, Calif.: Harcourt Brace Jovanovich, 1962.

Wolfgang Edelstein is director of research at the Max Planck Institute for Human Development and Education in Berlin, West Germany.

Kohlberg's work bridges the philosophical and psychological study of morality. Moral education programs should use the full complexity of issues and relate judgment and action.

Moral Education Beyond Moral Reasoning

Israel Scheffler

Kohlberg's important work has been enormously influential within psychology. What is more surprising is its effect on philosophy, where it has evoked numerous responses from philosophers of various schools, both in the United States and abroad. That many, perhaps most, of these responses have been critical is of small consequence. The interesting fact is that Kohlberg managed to stimulate a new level of exchange between the two fields, which I count as one of his most important achievements.

How did he accomplish this? Three elements of his work were mainly responsible. First, he systematically addressed a central area of life and thought—moral development. Second, he proposed serious and ambitious theses concerning such development. Finally, he acknowledged humanistic as well as scientific aspects of the subject, overriding conventional boundaries between the empirical and the philosophical, the descriptive and the normative, and the factual and the conceptual.

Philosophers were at once captivated by his boldness, challenged by his grand and simple vision, and charmed by his friendly willingness to engage in cross-disciplinary debate. Somewhat weary of the prevalent microscopic style of philosophizing, they were delighted to find a psychologist who propounded large doctrines affecting their own subject and claiming for such doctrines the authority of empirical inquiry. Cloistered metaethicists warily left their studies to scout the prospects of a collaborative effort by scientists and humanists to understand the nature of morality. Whatever the ultimate success of such effort, Kohlberg promoted it as an ideal worthy of pursuit in an increasingly distracted and fragmented world, badly in need of both morality and collaboration.

What Constitutes Moral Education?

Both the substance of Kohlberg's system and the responses to it have, however, grown more elaborate over the years. So much ink has by now been spilled in discussion of the fine points of this or that version of his theory that it would be unproductive for me to add to such discussion here. The nature and reality of his postulated moral stages, their presumed necessary and invariant order, the evidence for such order, the technique of his interviews, and the rationale of his scoring method have generated so much controversy and commentary, as well as internal alterations in response, that the system has presented a continuously moving target for skeptics and critics. Indeed, the methodological questions, in particular, have by now grown so complex that philosophers who initially relished Kohlberg's broad and simple vision of the subject now confront a prospect no less microscopic than their own.

I therefore gladly leave such questions of detail to my psychologist colleagues and address myself here to a broader question: What is the import of Kohlberg's work for moral education and what are its limitations? He stresses the preeminence of moral reasoning, the background principles and considerations that guide our moral judgments. In Socratic spirit, he emphasizes the role of knowledge of the good in the moral life; in Kantian spirit, he values consistency, universality, autonomy, and respect for persons.

These are certainly fundamental aspects of morality, and they fully deserve the critical role assigned to them in Kohlberg's scheme. The recent suggestion that an ethic of care is to be counterposed as an alternative to an ethic of principles has never seemed to me persuasive since respect for persons is a high, perhaps the highest, form of care, and care in any case needs to be apportioned equitably. It is worth recalling that Kant himself deduces the duty of helping those in need from his universalization principle; to promote a generally uncaring world, free of "love and sympathy," as he describes it, is, for him, a contradiction in the will.

Nevertheless, crucial as proper reasoning is to the moral life, and therefore to moral education, it has its natural limits. Indeed, nothing can substitute for such reasoning, yet it cannot stand alone. A full moral education requires other things in addition to appropriate reasoning, even if there is no question of such things replacing it. Moral education is thus, I believe, irreducible to moral development, under the particular construction given such development in Kohlberg's work.

I make this point about irreducibility not in criticism of his work as such—Kohlberg might conceivably have agreed with the thrust of my remarks—but rather to counteract the temptation to suppose that his work offers a complete account of moral education and a total guide to its practice. For this supposition of completeness, which is not in fact part of Kohlberg's doctrine, has unfortunately captured the public imagination, ever in search of educational panaceas.

What else, then, is required for moral education beyond proper moral reasoning? First, the establishment of basic forms of conduct; the foundations of character in action. Whatever their rationale, fundamental lines of decent behavior need to be laid down in practice and made second nature. The most sophisticated display of reasons will not redeem action that is habitually violent, deceptive, cruel, or contemptuous of others.

This Aristotelian point, in contrast to Kohlberg's Socratic view, is countered by his criticism of the "bag-of-virtues approach" which, he argues, is unclear because irremediably context-bound. But vices are, I suggest, much clearer than virtues, and minimally decent conduct, which avoids such vices as injury to others as well as self-harm, can and should be expected as a fundamental stratum of moral education. I want desperately to walk through the streets free of bodily assault and am comparatively less concerned with the moral stage of my law-abiding fellow citizens. Conversely, I am not much consoled if, having been stabbed, I am informed that my attacker is moving up the ladder of moral stage development.

More generally, conformity to basic social rules sanctioned by context is a prerequisite to taking hold of and modifying such rules later on. As in science and the arts, so in morality, acquisition of the inherited corpus is a base for further sophistication. Neither science nor art nor morality springs full-blown from the human mind. Without preliminary immersion in a tradition of practice—an appreciation of the force of its rules, obligations, rights, and demands—the concept of choice of actions and rules for oneself can hardly be achieved.

A second and related point bears not so much on Kohlberg's theory as on his method, which makes crucial use of the notion of dilemmas. Such use is theoretically benign, the intent being to elicit differences in the form of moral reasoning by application to hard cases. But the pernicious suggestion conveyed by such use is that moral behavior consists solely or primarily of hard cases, that is, brain teasers and conundrums to which there are no decisive answers, a suggestion that reinforces the very relativism Kohlberg sought to combat. As in the law, hard cases in morality must be conceived as presupposing a preponderance of easy cases, contingencies where decision poses no deep theoretical problems and where proper behavior is appropriately expected to be second nature. Here again, an Aristotelian emphasis is important.

Moral Education Is Not Ahistorical

The two points I have made so far might be roughly described as having to do with *moral content* as opposed to the form of moral conduct. My last point concerns *factual or historical content*. If the whole of moral education consisted in the attainment of some presumed highest stage of moral reasoning, culture and history should make no difference: Socrates and Kant should be equally well equipped morally no matter when or where they lived. But imagine them transplanted to twentieth-century Boston. They would be totally bewildered, not merely cognitively or factually but also morally. They would, I suggest, be not merely cognitively defective but also morally defective—morally handicapped in the extreme—being unaware of the very nature of the acts and alternatives presented daily to the contemporary agent in our society, and so unable fully to apply their principles to the great problems now confronting humanity. What could they possibly make of our commercial, industrial, or communications systems; of international finance; of multinational corporations; of international, political, and military rivalries; of guerrilla warfare; or of our ecological problems? The inescapable conclusion is that moral education cannot be skimmed off the top of history, or abstracted from its detail. You cannot be at once moral and ignorant. Facts have moral import.

Israel Scheffler is professor of philosophy in the Graduate School of Education Harvard University. His two most recent books are Of Human Potential *(1985) and* Inquiries: Philosophical Studies of Language, Science, and Learning *(1986).*

INDEX

Aboud, F., 24, 25, 28
Adelson, J., 97
Appearance-reality distinctions, and gender cognition, 15
Aristotle, 101
Arnold, M. L., 3
Aronfreed, J., 33, 47
Asch, S., 34, 47
Asia, gender categories in, 24

Baden, C., 3
Bailey, C., 55, 56
Balaban, T., 8, 20, 25, 29
Bandura, A., 11, 12, 15, 19, 32, 42-43, 44, 47
Batson, C. D., 55, 56
Bem, S. L., 6, 19, 24, 25, 28
Blasi, A., 2, 39, 40, 41, 47, 51-57
Block, J., 40, 47
Blum, L., 2, 59-69, 72
Bowman, L. L., 24, 29
Brown, M. E., 52, 57
Brown, R., 3, 71, 75
Brucken, L., 25, 28
Bruner, J. S., 96, 97
Bussey, K., 9-10, 11, 12, 15, 19, 20

Cambridge Commission for Nuclear Disarmament and Peace Education, 71-72
Cambridge Rindge and Latin Cluster School, 90
Candee, D., 40, 41, 47, 48, 53, 57
Carey, S., 24, 28
Carnegie-Mellon University, 89, 90, 91
Character traits, and moral action, 33, 41
Cheating behavior, and judgment-action relationship, 35-38
Children: under one, 12; at two, 8-9, 11, 16; at three, 7, 8-9, 11, 12, 14, 16, 17; at four, 7, 8-9, 11, 12, 15, 16, 17, 18; at five, 7, 8-9, 11, 15, 17, 18; at six, 7, 8-9, 17, 18; at seven, 7, 8, 9, 17, 18; at eight, 10, 18; at nine, 18, 72-75; at ten, 18, 84; at eleven, 84
Chomsky, N., 35, 47

Cleary, J., 71-76
Cognitive developmental theory: and gender category system, 22; and gender constancy, 10-11; and school reform, 96
Collman, P., 12, 18, 19
Conflict, moral education on, 72-75
Connecticut State Prison for Women, 78-79
Conservation, and gender constancy, 7, 16
Constantinople, A., 25, 28
Conventionalism, and universality, 60
Cooper, J., 8, 20, 25, 29
Cooperation, and moral development, 71
Cowan, G., 14, 19

Damon, W. M., 3, 18, 19, 39, 47
Danforth Foundation, 90
Davson-Galle, P., 59n
Deaux, K., 19, 26, 28
Defining attributes, and gender cognition, 14-15, 16
DeLisi, R., 9, 20
DeLucia, L. A., 7, 19
Development, as aim of education, 96
DeVries, R., 7, 13, 19
Dewey, J., 97
Dialogue, and universality and particularity, 66-67
Discourse, in just community, 84, 86
Duckworth, E., 2, 71-76
Duncker, K., 34, 47

Edelstein, W., 2, 71, 93-98
Elmendorf, D. M., 24, 28
Emmerich, W., 9, 19, 24, 28
Emotions: and motivation, 54-55; and particularity, 65

Fagot, B. I., 6, 19, 25, 28
Feldman, K. A., 52, 57
Fenton, E., 2, 89-92
Finn, C. E., Jr., 97
Fisher, K. W., 24, 28
Flanagan, O., Jr., 59n
Freire, P., 87

103

Freudian theory, 5, 22, 24
Freundlich, D., 40, 48
Frey, K. S., 8-9, 11, 20, 24, 25, 29
Fultz, J., 55, 56

Gelman, S. A., 12, 13, 16, 18, 19
Gender category system: aspects of, 21-29; characteristics of, 23-24; formulation of, 21-22; and self-socialization, 24-25; and sex-role flexibility, 26-28
Gender cognition: and gender identity, 12-17
Gender consistency, 9
Gender constancy: and gender identity, 7-12; and same-sex model imitation, 8-11, 15; sequential attainment of, 9; summary on, 16-17
Gender flexibility: and gender category system, 26-28; and gender identity, 17-19
Gender identity: aspects of, 5-20; background on theory of, 5-6; as constructed, 5-6; and gender cognition, 12-17; and gender constancy, 7-12; and gender flexibility, 17-19
Gender inferences, and gender cognition, 12
Gender salience, and gender flexibility, 17-19
Gender segregation, and gender flexibility, 18
Germany, just community of schools in, 81-85
Gilligan, C., 39, 47, 52
Goldman, K. S., 9, 19, 24, 28
Graham, P. A., 3
Graham, R., 90
Grim, P. F., 37, 47
Grinder, R. E., 37, 47

Haan, N., 32, 39, 40, 41, 47
Habermas, J., 59n, 60, 61, 65-68
Haflinger, 85, 87
Halverson, C. F., Jr., 9, 15, 20, 25, 28
Hampson, J. G., 7, 20
Hampson, J. L., 7, 20
Hartshorne, H., 33, 36, 37, 38, 48
Harvard University, 1, 3, 89, 90
Haugh, S. S., 14, 19
Havighurst, R. J., 33, 48, 49
Heingartner, A., 52, 57
Helwig, C., 45, 49

Hewer, A., 52, 57
Hickey, J., 40, 48, 78, 79, 80
Higgins, A., 3, 40, 47, 48, 67, 69
Hoffman, C. D., 14, 19
Hoffman, M. L., 55, 56-57
Hugo, V., 1
Hull, C. L., 5
Hume, D., 54, 57
Huston, A., 12, 17, 19, 21-22, 28

Iceland, school reform in, 96-97
Icelandic Psychological Association, 97
Imitation, of same-sex models, 8-11, 15, 25
Individuality, and particularity, 61-62
Integration, motivation as result of, 55-56
Internalization, and motivation, 56

Jacklin, C. N., 9, 12, 20, 25, 28
Jones, V., 33, 48
Judgment-action relationship: aspects of, 31-49; conclusions on, 46-47; correlational study of, 41; development in, 75; formulation of, 31-33; and group deliberations, 71; and immoral actions, 42-43; individual's structure of, 38, 42-43; and meaningfulness, 40-41; nonbehavioristic view of, 33-36; nonmoral, 41-42; philosophical analysis of, 39; and social situational contexts, 34-46; and stages, 37, 40, 41
Just community: background on, 81-82; and discourse, 84, 86; formulation of, 82-83; genesis of, 82; as long-term intervention, 84-85; and moral problems, 83-84; pedagogical principles underlying, 85; prison as, 77-80; and school reform, 86-87, 95; in school setting, 81-87; and teacher's ethos, 85-86

Kant, I., 64, 67, 100, 102
Kauffman, K., 2, 77-80
Keil, F. C., 13, 19
Kennedy, R. F., 38
Killen, M., 45, 47, 49
Kirsh, B., 9, 19, 24, 28
Kohlberg, L.: cited, 13, 20, 24, 28, 34, 35, 36, 37, 38, 39, 40, 41, 47, 48, 51, 52, 53, 56, 57, 60, 62, 63, 64, 65, 66,

67, 68-69, 79, 80, 87; criticisms of, 31-32, 46, 51, 52, 53, 62-68; educational legacy of, 81-87; and gender category system, 21-22, 24-26, 28; and gender identity, 5-10, 15-19; and judgment-action relationship, 31-41, 46-47; legacy of, 1-3; and moral education, 71-72, 75; and motivation, 51-56; and particularity, 59-60, 62-68; and philosophy, 99-101; and prison setting, 77-80; and Socratic paradox, 93-97; and teacher education, 89-92
Korczak, J., 87
Krebs, D., 39, 48
Krebs, R., 37, 48
Kuhn, D., 25, 28

Lehrer, L., 37, 48
Letourneau, K. J., 25, 29
Levine, C., 52, 57
Lewin, K., 34, 48
Little, J. K., 25, 28
Loevinger, J., 52

Maccoby, E. E., 2, 5-20, 21, 22, 23, 25, 26, 28
McConaghy, M. J., 24, 28
Mahapatra, M., 60, 69
Major, B., 19, 26, 28
Marcus, D. E., 15, 20
Markman, E., 13, 19
Martin, C. L., 9, 15, 20, 25, 28
Massachusetts, prison officers in, 77-78
May, M. S., 33, 36, 37, 38, 48
Mayer, R., 87
Mead, M., 23, 29
Meehan, J., 59*n*
Merriman, W. E., 24, 29
Milgram, S., 40, 44-45, 48
Miller, J., 60, 69
Mischel, H. N., 42, 48
Mischel, W., 42, 48
Money, J., 7, 20
Montessori, M., 87
Moral action. *See* Judgment-action relationship
Moral development, and motivation, 51-57
Moral domain, and judgment-action relationship, 43-46
Moral education: aspects of, 71-102; case study of, 95-97; classroom example of, 71-76; on conflict, 72-75; constituents of, 100-101; essence of, 75; historical and factual content of, 101-102; and moral reasoning, 99-102; in prison setting, 77-80; and schools as just community, 81-87; substance and method paradox in, 93-98; and teacher education, 89-92
Moral judgment. *See* Judgment-action relationship
Morality: complementary principles of, 59-62; epistemological realm of, 35-36, 39, 40, 42, 44; and exceptions to rules, 64-65; gadfly for, 94-95; in public and private domains, 64; and tragedy, 94; understanding as basis of, 51; universality and particularity in, 59-69
Motivation: analysis of, 51-57; and emotions, 54-55; and integration, 55-56; moral, 51-53; and reasoning, 52-53, 56; and stages, 51-52

Nash, S. C., 25, 28
National Science Foundation, 91
Natural-kinds constancy, and gender cognition, 13-14
Need, recognition of, and particularity, 61-62, 67-68
Nixon, R. M., 40, 89
Noam, G., 3
Noddings, N., 64, 69
Nunner-Winkler, G., 63

Obedience, and judgment-action relationship, 40, 44-46
Oser, F. K., 2, 81-87, 95, 96, 98
Overton, W. F., 15, 20

Particularity: analysis of, 59-69; and applications, 65; concept of, 60-61; conclusion on, 68; and individuality, 61-62; and morality, 62-68; and stages, 59-60, 62, 66-67; universality complementary to, 59-62
Patry, 85, 87
Peck, R. F., 33, 49
Percival, T. Q., 52, 57
Perry, D. G., 9-10, 11, 20
Perry, L. C., 11, 20

Personal relationships, and morality, 62-64
Pestalozzi, J. H., 87
Philosophy: and judgment and action, 39; and moral reasoning, 99-102
Piaget, J., 1, 7, 16, 22, 31, 32-33, 34, 35, 38, 40, 49, 71, 75, 94, 97
Plato, 93, 94, 97
Power, C., 40, 49
Power, F. C., 67, 69
Prison, as just community, 77-80
Pritchard, M. S., 52, 57
Psychoanalytic theory, and gender constancy, 10-11

Quarfoth, G. R., 24, 29

Rationalism, and morality, 64-65
Reasoning: and emotions, 54; and motivation, 52-53, 56
Reinforcement: and gender identity, 6; and self-socialization, 25
Rich, J. M., 54, 57
Robinson, J., 9, 15, 20
Rosenwald, A., 39, 48
Ruble, D. N., 8, 20, 25, 29

Same-sex models: and gender constancy, 8-11, 15; and self-socialization, 25
Scharf, P., 40, 48, 78, 79, 80
Scheffler, I., 2-3, 71, 99-102
Schelhas-Miller, C., 27, 29
Schoenrade, P. A., 55, 56
Schools: just community in, 81-87; and moral problems, 83-84; reform of, 86-87, 95
Schrader, D., 1-3
Schwartz, S. H., 52, 57
Schweder, R., 60, 69
Self-socialization, and gender category system, 24-25
Selman, R. L., 3, 39, 47, 49
Serbin, L. A., 17-18, 20
Sex-role development: and gender category system, 22; and gender constancy, 7-8; and gender identity, 5-20
Sharabany, R., 9, 19, 24, 28
Siegal, M., 9, 15, 20
Sirhan, S., 38
Skinner, B. F., 5

Slaby, R. G., 2, 8-9, 11, 20, 21-29
Smedslund, J., 7, 20
Smetana, J. G., 25, 29, 39, 44, 46, 47, 49
Smith, M. B., 40, 47
Social learning theory: and gender category system, 22; and gender identity, 5-6, 9-10, 11; and judgment-action relationship, 33, 42-43
Social situational contexts, judgment and action in, 34-46
Socrates, 2, 93-95, 97, 100, 101, 102
Sprafkin, C., 17-18, 20
Stages: judgment and action at, 37, 40, 41; motivation at, 51-52; particularity at, 59-60, 62, 66-67; in prison setting, 79
Stone Foundation, 89
Straughan, R., 53, 57
Switzerland, schools in, 83

Taba, H., 33, 48, 96, 98
Teachers: education of, 89-92; ethos of, 85-86
Temporal stability, and gender constancy, 9
Tension reduction, and motivation, 55
Thoreau, H. D., 38
Thought processes, and moral action, 34
Trautner, H. M., 15, 20
Triviz, R. M., 25, 29
Turiel, E., 2, 31-49

Universality: and conventionalism, 60; and particularity, 59-69; and personal relations, 63

Virtue, concept of, 93

Washington University, 90
Wehren, A., 9, 20
White, A. V., 11, 20
White, S. H., 37, 47
Wilson, E., 38
Wong, D., 59n

Yale University, 32-33, 40
Young, I., 67, 69

Zutavern, 85, 87

Ordering Information

NEW DIRECTIONS FOR CHILD DEVELOPMENT is a series of paperback books that presents the latest research findings on all aspects of children's psychological development, including their cognitive, social, moral, and emotional growth. Books in the series are published quarterly, in Fall, Winter, Spring, and Summer, and are available for purchase by subscription as well as by single copy.

SUBSCRIPTIONS for 1989-90 cost $48.00 for individuals (a savings of 20 percent over single-copy prices) and $64.00 for institutions, agencies, and libraries. Please do not send institutional checks for personal subscriptions. Standing orders are accepted.

SINGLE COPIES cost $14.95 when payment accompanies order. (California, New Jersey, New York, and Washington, D.C., residents please include appropriate sales tax.) Billed orders will be charged postage and handling.

DISCOUNTS FOR QUANTITY ORDERS are available. Please write to the address below for information.

ALL ORDERS must include either the name of an individual or an official purchase order number. Please submit your order as follows:
 Subscriptions: specify series and year subscription is to begin
 Single copies: include individual title code (such as CD1)

MAIL ALL ORDERS TO:
 Jossey-Bass Inc., Publishers
 350 Sansome Street
 San Francisco, California 94104

OTHER TITLES AVAILABLE IN THE
NEW DIRECTIONS FOR CHILD DEVELOPMENT SERIES
William Damon, Editor-in-Chief

CD46 Economic Stress: Effects on Family Life and Child Development, *Vonnie C. McLoyd, Constance Flanagan*
CD45 Infant Stress and Coping, *Michael Lewis, John Worobey*
CD44 Empathy and Related Emotional Responses, *Nancy Eisenberg*
CD43 Maternal Responsiveness: Characteristics and Consequences, *Marc H. Bornstein*
CD42 Black Children and Poverty: A Developmental Perspective, *Diana T. Slaughter*
CD41 Children's Mathematics, *Geoffrey B. Saxe, Maryl Gearhart*
CD40 Parental Behavior in Diverse Societies, *Robert A. LeVine, Patrice M. Miller, Mary Maxwell West*
CD39 Developmental Psychopathology and Its Treatment, *Ellen D. Nannis, Philip A. Cowan*
CD38 Children's Gender Schemata, *Lynn S. Liben, Margaret L. Signorella*
CD37 Adolescent Social Behavior and Health, *Charles E. Irwin, Jr.*
CD36 Symbolic Development in Atypical Children, *Dante Cicchetti, Marjorie Beeghly*
CD35 How Children and Adolescents View the World of Work, *John H. Lewko*
CD34 Maternal Depression and Infant Disturbance, *Edward Z. Tronick, Tiffany Field*
CD33 Children's Intellectual Rights, *David Moshman*
CD32 Early Experience and the Development of Competence, *William Fowler*
CD31 Temperament and Social Interaction in Infants and Children, *Jacqueline V. Lerner, Richard M. Lerner*
CD30 Identity in Adolescence: Processes and Contents, *Alan S. Waterman*
CD27 The Development of Reading Skills, *Thomas H. Carr*
CD24 Children in Families Under Stress, *Anna-Beth Doyle, Dolores Gold, Debbie S. Moscowitz*
CD22 Adolescent Development in the Family, *Harold D. Grotevant, Catherine R. Cooper*
CD19 Children and Divorce, *Lawrence A. Kurdek*
CD14 Children's Conceptions of Health, Illness, and Bodily Functions, *Roger Bibace, Mary E. Walsh*
CD9   Children's Play, *Kenneth H. Rubin*